The

LAST
MONOPOLY

Privatizing the Postal Service
for the Information Age

EDITED BY
EDWARD L. HUDGINS

CATO
INSTITUTE
Washington, D.C.

Library of Congress Cataloging-in-Publication Data

The last monopoly : privatizing the postal service for the information
  age / edited by Edward L. Hudgins.
     p.   cm.
  Papers presented at the Cato Institute conference, held June 14, 1995,
in Washington, D.C.
  Includes bibliographical references and index.
  ISBN 1-882577-31-0. — ISBN 1-882577-32-9 (pbk.)
    1. United States Postal Service—Congresses. 2. Postal service—
United States—Congresses. 3. Privatization—United States—
Congresses. I. Hudgins, Edward Lee, 1952– . II. Cato Institute.
HE6371.L37   1996
353.0087'3—dc20   96-30393
                                                                   CIP

Cover Design by Mark Fondersmith.

Printed in the United States of America.

CATO INSTITUTE
1000 Massachusetts Ave., N.W.
Washington, D.C. 20001

Contents

PART IV PRIVATIZATION PLANS

Acknowledgments

The Cato Institute conference, "Private Postal Service in the 21st Century," held June 14, 1995, in Washington, D.C., which resulted in the papers in this book, was conducted with the generous assistance of the Shelby Cullom Davis Foundation and the Figurehut Companies.

I also wish to acknowledge and thank those who hosted panels at the conference. Cato's executive vice president, David Boaz, who has written on postal privatization, is a leading market liberal thinker. Edited books to his credit include *Left, Right, and Baby Boom* and (with Edward H. Crane) *An American Vision: Policies for the '90s* and *Market Liberalism: A Paradigm for the 21st Century*. Ronald D. Utt served as the associate director for privatization at the U.S. Office of Management and Budget during the Reagan administration, and is better known as the first and, so far, only privatization czar. He also was executive vice president of the National Chamber Foundation, the research and education division of the U.S. Chamber of Commerce. Cato chairman and *Regulation* magazine editor William A. Niskanen was a member of the Council of Economic Advisers from 1981 to 1985, including nine months as acting chairman. He was assistant director of the Office of Management and Budget from 1970 to 1972.

Burt Ely, president of Ely & Company, Inc., a financial institutions consulting firm, also deserves mention. Although his conference presentation does not appear in this volume, Ely is a longtime advocate of postal privatization and the author of "Privatizing the Postal Service: Why Do It; How to Do It," in *Free the Mail*, published by the Cato Institute and edited by Peter J. Ferrara.

Patricia Felder, the administrative assistant to Cato's regulatory studies staff, did yeoman's work entering the frequent changes and edits for this volume.

OVERVIEW
THE LAST MONOPOLY:
Privatizing the Postal Service for the Information Age

PART I
THE STATE OF THE POSTAL SERVICE

Chapter 1: The View from the U.S. Postal Service
Marvin T. Runyon

The U.S. Postmaster General, while acknowledging problems with the Postal Service, maintains that subjecting it to standard business practices will make it function more efficiently. He offers as a model the federal government's Tennessee Valley Authority, which he administered in the 1980s.

Runyon asserts that universal mail service "backed by the full faith and trust of the United States government" is necessary to bind the nation together. He believes that "the right amount of deregulation" will allow the Postal Service to "compete on an equal footing with other couriers and alternative communication, while still ensuring service to all Americans."

Chapter 2: The Postal Monopoly Law: A Historical Perspective
James I. Campbell Jr.

Campbell traces the history of America's postal monopoly from its origin in a temporary decree in 1635 by King Charles I of England. The Post Office originally asserted a monopoly over *letters* and *packets* transported over government post roads between postal offices along these routes. With the advent of steamboats and railroads in the early 1800s, private express companies began carrying mail by these means. In response, Congress in 1845 suppressed private delivery.

Originally the Post Office carried only intercity mail between postal stations. But as private companies began providing local delivery within cities, the Post Office in 1872 obtained from Congress a monopoly over that service as well.

Campbell documents how throughout its history the government-backed postal monopoly has expanded its jurisdiction over items such as commercial documents by expanding the definitions of *letters* and *packets*.

Chapter 3: Postal Service Problems: The Need to Free the Mails
Peter J. Ferrara

As evidence of the inherent problems of the government postal monopoly, Ferrara suggests that current Postal Service rates are as much as 50 percent higher than they would be if competition were allowed.

Critics claim that eliminating the monopoly would reduce or eliminate service in rural areas or boost prices. While Ferrara asserts there is no reason to shield rural residents from the true costs of delivery, the uniform pricing and universal service by private package delivery companies probably would be applied to first- and third-class mail if markets were freed. Ferrara suggests that the mail monopoly be lifted first in rural areas to allow competition for the market that critics claim would be neglected by private carriers.

Critics complain of restrictions on the Postal Service's control over its rates, services, and labor practices. Ferrara says the answer is not in bureaucratic reforms. It is competition and an elimination of the postal monopoly.

Chapter 4: Mass Mailer Problems
Gene Del Polito

Mail marketers and advertisers find that the Postal Service cannot provide timely and reliable universal service at market prices. Del Polito compares the problems of the Postal Service with an immuno-deficiency disease. While the symptoms often are treated, if the disease remains, the patient will continue to decline. Postmasters general from time to time announce improvements in the quality of postal services. But Del Polito maintains that this is to be expected, since throwing resources at symptoms often brings temporary relief. But the deeper disease in the system remains.

Illustrative of the problem is the fact that a mail carrier who finishes his route in less than the allotted time is given more work. A less competent colleague who does not complete assignments can receive overtime pay. The incentives of the Postal Service guarantee problems. Only a fundamental change in the current system can save universal delivery.

PART II
COMPETING WITH THE POSTAL SERVICE

Chapter 5: Competing Carriers
Thomas M. Lenard

Supporters of the postal monopoly often claim that in local delivery the huge U.S. Postal Service is far better able to provide services at a lower cost than small, private operations. But private carriers are allowed to deliver "unaddressed" advertising mail—such as circulars, catalogs, and periodicals—that are distributed to most addresses in an area. This material is similar to addressed third-class mail, over which the Postal Service has a monopoly.

Lenard's survey of small private operations with annual revenues between $2 million and $20 million finds that 80 percent of their jobs cost less than comparable Postal Service jobs. Private firm costs on average were only 73 percent of the costs for government-carried third-class mail. The Postal Service handled about $8.2 billion in third-class mail in the year of Lenard's survey. Assuming that this mail is overpriced at the rate found in the survey, Lenard suggests that customers paid $2.5 billion in higher prices than if private carriers had delivered third-class mail.

Chapter 6: E-mail, Faxes, and Personal Computers:
Telecommunications Alternatives
Stephen L. Gibson

Gibson echoes a theme found in many of the chapters in this volume. The contrast between the sweeping information and telecommunications revolution and the plodding-to-stagnant Postal Service could not be more stark. Gibson observes that the 10-millionfold explosion in the capacity to process and transmit information electronically dwarfs the thousandfold increase brought about by the introduction of the printing press. E-mail, faxes, and cellular phones already have changed the nature of communications. Personal computers have spawned the Internet and World Wide Web.

Gibson notes that so far electronic communication and information storage have not replaced the paper-based system of which the Postal

Service is a key component. But he observes by analogy that for the first 40 years of the Industrial Revolution, huge, centrally located steam engines powered electric equipment in factories. Major productivity gains came only as factories were redesigned around individual machines with built-in engines. As communications systems in the future are designed around new technical capacities, paper messages, along with the Postal Service, could well disappear.

Chapter 7: Natural Monopoly Myths: Lessons for Postal Service
Thomas J. DiLorenzo

Proponents often claim that first- and third-class mail delivery must be the exclusive business of a single provider because it is a "natural monopoly." But as DiLorenzo explains, this argument originally was used for utilities such as electricity, gas, spectrum broadcasting, and cable television. Supposedly, one large supplier can provide services at a lower cost than many smaller ones. Competition would hike prices and reduce services.

But DiLorenzo points out that at the turn of the century private-sector competition in utilities held down prices to consumers. In 1887 New York City had six electric light companies, and in 1907 in Chicago, 45 had the right to operate. Monopolies were special favors to politically powerful companies.

In recent decades local governments have established monopolies for cable television companies. But where competition is allowed, consumers benefit. Faced with competition, Cablevision of Central Florida reduced its basic monthly rate from $12.95 to $6.50. Competition in Presque Ilse, Maine, caused the incumbent supplier to upgrade from 12 to 54 channels.

Today deregulation and competition are found in all utilities that have been labeled "natural monopolies." This suggests that mail delivery would be less costly and more reliable if the Postal Service's monopoly is eliminated.

PART III

MARKET STRUCTURES FOR PRIVATE DELIVERY

Chapter 8: Patterns of Private Delivery
R. Richard Geddes

The U.S. Postal Service is a highly vertically integrated operation, with its trucks that pick up mail, facilities that sort it, and carriers who deliver it. Geddes suggests that with removal of the government monopoly on first-class mail delivery, the postal market likely would be stratified by speed of delivery, with competition in each stratum and a high level of overall reliability for all deliveries. Already, competition is permitted in overnight delivery, though the government mandates high prices for this service. Without this mandate, prices might drop but still would be higher than for lower-priority, and thus lower-priced, delivery.

Geddes also maintains that companies providing the swiftest service would be more vertically integrated, since they would need the tightest control over delivery schedules. Companies offering slower and lower-priced delivery would rely on contracting out to keep costs low. Thus, if the monopoly on first- and third-class mail delivery were repealed, consumers would have even greater choices in the speed of delivery and price levels to suit their needs.

Chapter 9: Competition in Postal Service: International
Perspectives
Michael A. Crew

Crew finds that governments in most industrialized countries are moving their postal services in the direction of market models. Most have converted their state-owned and -operated systems into public corporations, which have some flexibility but cannot seek profits. Others are converting such corporations into public limited corporations. These are organized like private firms, with wide autonomy over their own operations and the rights to make profits and issue stock. But with the exception of Sweden and Finland, governments still mandate monopolies over certain classes of mail.

Crew discusses how high labor costs and the need for access to established postal networks will be the principal issues to be addressed in any move towards postal privatization.

Chapter 10: Problems with Privatization
Murray Comarow

The former senior assistant postmaster general and executive director of the presidential commission that devised the 1970 postal reorganization plan suggests that a new commission analyze the problems with the Postal Service and recommend changes.

Comarow observes that for its size and compared with postal services in other countries, the U.S. Postal Service operates well. But he also acknowledges the serious problems with the current system. Still, Comarow cautions against calls for privatization based on ideology without adequate concern for the details about how a private system would operate.

PART IV

PRIVATIZATION PLANS

Chapter 11: Employee Ownership of the Postal Service
Rep. Dana Rohrabacher

Representative Rohrabacher (R-Calif.) sees resistance from postal unions and employees as a major barrier to privatizing the U.S. Postal Service. His solution is make the Postal Service an employee stock-ownership company. This would give postal employees an opportunity to profit from a new, competitive private firm.

In legislation he has introduced in the House of Representatives, Rohrabacher would give the new employee-owned service a five-year grace period before competition from private delivery services would be allowed. That would give the private Postal Service time to restructure and make itself competitive. Rohrabacher maintains that such an approach would bring higher quality service at competitive rates to postal customers.

Chapter 12: Breaking Up the Postal Service
Douglas K. Adie

Adie maintains that if a privatized Postal Service remains a single entity, it would still have too much control of the postal market and could use its assets, accumulated as a government monopoly, to cripple competitors. Further, he does not believe that public assets paid for by taxpayers and captive consumers should be turned over to postal workers. Adie's solution: break up the Postal Service the way American Telephone and Telegraph's local operations were broken up into regional, Bell telephone systems.

Adie would create five regional divisions and one parcel-post company. In addition, a holding company would be created for other divisions until they are sold off, helping to assign assets and personnel, and carrying out the other steps to privatization. This holding company then might transform itself to provide support services for the newly privatized companies.

Introduction: A Private Postal Service for the 21st Century

Edward L. Hudgins

While fast, efficient communications are vital for advanced industrial economies and societies, the United States is poised to enter the 21st century with a postal monopoly established in the 18th.

The federal government maintains a monopoly on the transport and delivery of messages on pieces of paper or other material media. It is a federal crime for private suppliers to offer these services. Yet problems with the U.S. Postal Service (USPS) are chronic. More and more, the defects of the Postal Service stand in contrast to the successes of the private sector-created telecommunications revolution. Critics compare e-mail with what they call the Postal Service's snail mail. The situation suggests that the days of the Postal Service as a government monopoly may and certainly should be numbered.

An Economic Anomaly

A cursory look at the complex technological society around us refutes the claims that only the federal government can provide swift, high-quality, cost-effective mail delivery, and that the private sector somehow is not up to the task. Private airlines safely convey passengers from all parts of the country to disparate destinations. (The major causes of delays are the government-owned and -operated airports and air traffic control system.) Trucks and trains transport perishable food, delicate consumer goods, costly industrial equipment, and fragile furnishings to customers in every corner of the country. Why, then, do supporters of the government postal monopoly believe that private entrepreneurs cannot successfully transport messages on paper door to door?

The author is director of regulatory studies at the Cato Institute and senior editor of *Regulation* magazine.

The prices of products and services drop when markets and economic freedom force suppliers to become more efficient. Airlines were deregulated beginning in the late 1970s; as a result, the cost of air travel per passenger mile, adjusted for inflation, has dropped by at least half. Truck transportation was deregulated at about the same time; the savings in transport costs, passed along in lower prices for many products being transported, is estimated as high as $100 billion over a decade. As important, reliable efficient tranportation allowed the development of just-in-time inventory systems that allowed enterprises to increase their productivity.

The newest information transmission and processing sector, a result of private sector innovations, consists of millions of personal computers as well as as mainframes connected by the Internet. In 1981 the first personal computers came with 64 kilobytes of memory and sold for $3,000, or about $46,000 per megabyte. Today a megabyte of memory in a computer can be had for under $1. Why, then, has the price for sending first-class mail not gone down? Why have stamp prices risen nine times since 1973, from 8 cents to 32 cents today? The Postal Service's chief financial officer, Michael J. Riley, defends the USPS record: "If we had not automated [at a cost of over $600 million in the late 1980s] we would have had an $8 billion price increase, instead of a $5 billion increase [represented in the 32 cent rate]."[1]

Of course, where competition with the Postal Service is allowed, as in overnight delivery, the private sector prospers and the USPS simply is not a significant supplier. Also of interest is the fact that federal law mandates that private-sector prices for the service must be at least $3 or twice the cost of the first-class mail equivalent. Yet customers pay the price, indicating a preference for the private-sector guarantee of delivery over the government's less-reliable monopoly, even if it costs 10 or 20 times more than a stamp.

Efficiency: Lost in the Mails

The country was shocked in recent years by tales of Postal Service incompetence. Inspectors at the South Maryland processing facility found 2.3 million pieces of bulk mail delayed for up to nine days and 800,000 pieces of first-class mail delayed for three days.[2] The mail was stashed in tractor-trailer trucks—apparently because it is not counted in postal statistics as "delayed" if it is not actually in the facility. Naturally this calls into question the reliability of other Postal Service statistics and claims of improved efficiency based on them. One suburban Washington, D.C., mail carrier was found to have bags of mail stored in his apartment with corpses of animals.

In Chicago in 1994, 5.9 million pieces of forwarded mail were delayed for a month. A hundred bags of months-old mail were found in one truck; 200 pounds of burned mail were found under a viaduct.[3]

In that same year in the Bronx, New York, a private high school principal found that mail sent to other parts of the city was taking two weeks to reach its destination. Documents that were 13 days in transit to a Manhattan destination a few miles away caused the school to miss budget deadlines, costing it $7,000.[4]

Such incidents have brought pressure on the Postal Service from angry customers and members of Congress. Rep. Steny H. Hoyer (D-Md.) said, "The bottom line is we are outraged about the persistence of poor mail delivery service in this region."[5]

Postmaster General Marvin T. Runyon has vowed to reverse the Postal Service's poor record and make it operate more like a business. And of late there have been no major scandals of the magnitude of those in Washington and Chicago. Further, USPS figures show a 4 percent improvement nationally over the past year in next-day delivery, up to 88 percent of test letters mailed.[6]

But a striking pattern with the Postal Service is its roller-coaster drops and improvements in quality. Each postmaster general pledges to improve mail services and hold down costs. Some do, for a time. But problems and price hikes always come back.

In many ways this is not surprising. The average wage and benefit package of clerks and sorters is nearly $43,000, compared to about $35,000 for all private sector workers.[7] The Postal Rate Commission found recently that "nonproductive time" constitutes 28.4 percent of mail-processing labor costs. There is 1 manager for every 10 workers at the USPS, compared with 1 for every 15 workers at Federal Express.

Of course, the facts that there are 800,000 mostly unionized postal workers and that the USPS is a protected monopoly combine to create an economic dynamic that almost ensures periodic cost and quality crises. There are very few hardships for the Postal Service if quality suffers, since customers cannot turn to competitors for services. But it is politically very difficult for the Postal Service to cut its work force to hold down costs. One cause of this difficulty is the fact that all congressional districts have numerous post offices and postal workers to remind elected officials and candidates of their special interests. Another cause is the fact that postal union political action committees make generous contributions to political campaigns, $3.27 million for the 1993–1994 election cycle.[8]

If the Postal Service were subject to competition, it is likely that quality would not have sunk so low nor prices continued to rise. The situation probably would not have reached a crisis, with customers inconvenienced and policymakers outraged, before action was taken. With competition, as quality declined, consumers would start switching to alternative suppliers. The Postal Service would have a choice: act quickly to correct its problems, or lose its customers and either shut down or be bought out by competitors.

Public-Private Convergence?

Some of the techniques available to or used by the Postal Service to improve quality and contain costs call into question the claim that a postal monopoly is needed. These techniques are used in the private sector, thus suggesting that they would be used without a government monopoly. For example, to hold down costs, the USPS offers discounts for businesses that presort mail going to different cities, and allows transportation of such presorted bags by private trucks to post offices in the cities of destination. The USPS also offers discounts on bar-coded mail. In early 1996 the Postal Rate Commission, a government body that must approve prices for mail services, endorsed a plan to offer even more substantial discounts for large business mailers using such techniques. But why not contract out all bulk shipments between major distribution centers, or all mail sorting to private suppliers, or simply allow the private sector to perform those functions entirely?

The Postal Service used to claim as one of its virtues that it delivers door to door. Yet in 1978 it decided that no service would be provided to the doors of newly built residences. Roadside boxes are used where appropriate. But increasingly the Postal Service delivers to cluster boxes in housing developments. Cluster boxes allow carriers to serve dozens of customers in a fraction of the time it takes to go door to door. Now individuals must travel as far as half a mile to retrieve their mail. Private suppliers, if allowed to deliver mail, might find it profitable to offer delivery to the door for no extra charge in densely populated areas. Many customers might be willing to pay a fee for such convenience.

But the lines between the USPS and the private sector are becoming blurred. More and more, a trek of a half mile or less brings one to private establishments such as Mail Boxes, Etc., that offer mailboxes for rent at offices in shopping centers and other locations convenient to customers. Even with postal boxes for rent in government post offices, customers often choose private-sector alternatives. So why not allow private carriers to deliver to government cluster boxes in housing developments or to establish their own boxes in such locations?

All the functions performed by the Postal Service are being performed well at some level by the private sector. And to the extent that the Postal Service turns to contracting with the private sector as a means to increase efficiency, the more it advertises that others can do its job.

Self-Promotion and Power Seeking

The Postal Service has taken steps to polish its tarnished image. Like a typical bureaucracy, it is engaging in heavy self-promotion, advertisements not about the services it offers but simply about itself, to protect its existence as a monopoly.

Many critics were dismayed when, with scandals breaking in 1994, the Postal Service announced it was spending $7 million to develop a new logo. That should have been no surprise. After all, the USPS is the monopoly that spent $90 million for advertising in the 1992 Olympics in Barcelona, Spain, and Albertville, France.[9] It is doubtful that the USPS increased its business through the ads. After all, Americans, and for that matter Spaniards and French citizens, could hardly be induced to switch to the Postal Service from competing carriers because no competitors are allowed.

In late 1995 the USPS paid for a series of radio commercials that featured actor George C. Scott extolling its virtues. Scott explains that the price of stamps goes up because the Postal Service does not receive government funds and operates solely on receipts from customers. But this information is misleading. Total postal revenues in fiscal 1996 are estimated at $56 billion. In that year the federal

Table 1
FEDERAL OUTLAYS TO THE POSTAL SERVICE
(in billions of dollars)

	1985	1986	1987	1988	1989	1990	1991	1992	1993	1994
Total	1.35	.758	1.59	2.23	.13	2.12	1.83	1.17	1.60	1.23
On budget	1.35	.758	1.59	2.23	.44	.49	.51	.51	.16	.13
Off budget	—	—	—	—	−.31	1.63	1.32	.66	1.40	1.10

The Budget for Fiscal Year 1995, Historical Tables, p. 46, and *The Budget for Fiscal Year 1996,* p. 1044–45.

government will give an estimated $770.9 million to the Postal Service, with $625 million of the sum listed as off budget and $145.9 million on budget. Of the on-budget expenditures, $109.1 is principally to offset revenues forgone on federally mandated free or reduced-rate mail such as Congress's franking privileges. Subsidies to the Postal Service have fluctuated over the past decade, hitting a high of $2.23 billion in 1988. (See Table 1.)

In past years the Postal Service has run deficits. What George C. Scott does *not* mention in the commercials is that the Postal Service has special preferential borrowing privileges with the federal government. He does *not* mention that the monopoly power of the Postal Service to jack up stamp prices without fear of customers' turning to competitors is a kind of government-backed power to tax. He does *not* mention that stamp prices might go down, as do the prices of many other goods and services, if the Postal Service were subject to competition. He does *not* mention that the USPS has billions of dollars in unfunded pension liabilities backed by the federal government, that is, by American taxpayers. He does *not* mention that, unlike private enterprises, the Postal Service is exempt from most taxes.

Why is the quasi-government agency wasting money not on advertising its services but simply on boosting its image? Perhaps part of the answer is to counteract the embarrassing content of the actual advertisements for its services. One is for "Priority Mail." Several years ago this was guaranteed two-day priority mail, for $2.90. But in 1995 the ads read "Are you paying for tomorrow when the day after is so much cheaper? Priority Mail. 2-day delivery* within your region, starting at $3." And what does one find at the bottom of the page under the asterisk? "*Average two-day performance within the region shown. Delivery measured from post office to post office excluding time of delivery to address. Such performance is an average, not a guarantee. Delivery outside a region may take longer."[10]

This is in sharp contrast to ads by the private Federal Express proclaiming "When it absolutely, positively, must be there," or "We can deliver before 8:00 a.m., or by 10:30 a.m., or by 4:00 p.m. etc."

The Postal Service recently did decide to stop one form of advertisement. It will no longer publicize the results of customer surveys. Apparently the less-than-perfect results do not create the image the Postal Service is cultivating.

Yet the Postal Service does have time and money to engage in enterprises that have absolutely nothing to do with delivering the mails. It has gone into the business of marketing prepaid phone calling cards for long-distance calls. Provision of the cards of course is not part of mail delivery. The Postal Service uses its assets and facilities gained from its monopoly position to compete with private-sector suppliers.

But the Postal Service is notorious for attempting to grab any market it can. In the late 1970s it tried to assert its monopoly control over mail to ban the use of the newly emerging technology of electronic mail. Fortunately it was overruled.[11]

The Darker Side of Monopoly

Customers standing in long lines at a post office, listening to clerks in back rooms talking and laughing while only one or two clerks provide service, probably would concede that the USPS is inefficient. But they might be surprised to learn that the monopoly that employs kindly carriers delivering postcards to Grandma also maintains its power and control at the expense of civil liberties.

Traditionally, government control over the mails has been used to silence communications of which political authorities did not approve. Before the Civil War anti-slavery material in the mails would be stopped in certain parts of the country. Under the Comstock Act of 1873, material deemed "obscene, lewd or lascivious" was banned from the mails. Birth control information was kept out of postal circulation. In 1912 postal officials refused to allow mailings of a newspaper article by feminist Margaret Sanger entitled "What

Every Girl Should Know" because it contained the words "gonor-
rhea" and "syphilis."[12] Works of literature by authors such as D. H.
Lawrence, Theodore Dreiser, and Edmund Wilson were suppressed.
In this century material defined as "obscene" has been targeted by
postal inspectors.

In 1993 the Postal Service stepped up efforts against businesses
that "misused" such overnight couriers as Federal Express. It
claimed that some enterprises were illegally bypassing the Postal
Service by using private providers for communications not deemed
"urgent."

How does the USPS know of these "misuses"? A businessperson
seals a document in a FedEx envelope, FedEx accepts the envelope
and transports it to its destination, and the recipient opens it. Does
the government place spies in the mailroom in the sender's office
or do federal agents pose as secretaries working for the recipient?
In fact, armed postal agents have conducted inspections and audits
of records in private firms and, over a three-year period, levied half
a million dollars in fines. Postal inspectors also conduct surveillance,
with binoculars and telescopes, of shipments and delivery trucks to
collect evidence or count the volume of "misuse" of couriers.

The Cato Institute itself experienced a small sample of postal
intimidation regarding its postal service conference in 1988. The
advertising material for the conference featured a variation of the
postal "eagle" logo, though with significant changes. Cato president
Edward H. Crane received a letter (with the salutation "Dear Mr.
Cato") from a Postal Service lawyer, warning of the dire consequences of logo copyright infringement.

Another case of abuse concerned a direct-mail marketer, Benjamin
Suarez, who distributes sweepstakes-type promotionals similar to
those of Publishers Clearing House. In December 1994 the Postal
Service obtained a Temporary Detention Order against Suarez's
business, claiming that four promotionals were fraudulent. This
meant that during the busy Christmas season, the USPS seized and
held all mail addressed to Suarez's enterprise, with no explanation
sent to customers, and with no way for the enterprise to inform
customers what had happened to their money and requests.

A hearing was held in February 1995 before a federal judge on
whether to make the Temporary Detention Order "preliminary,"
that is, to keep it in effect until the case could be resolved, potentially

for months or even years. Such preliminary injunctions are routinely granted. But at the hearing, part of the Postal Service's concerns about Suarez became clear. In the materials that the postal inspector submitted to the judge were pages from Suarez's book, *Seven Steps to Freedom II*, that were extremely critical of the Postal Service, as well as sections critical of federal judges. Excerpts included the "laws under which the U.S. Postal Service operates are unconstitutional and constitute mock justice,"[13] and "The USPS administrative court is rigged."[14] Suarez further wrote:

> The U.S. Federal Court System is also rigged in the USPS's favor—the USPS wins virtually 100% of the time in temporary restraining orders (TROs), injunctions and appeal suits on USPS administrative court decisions.[15]

Suarez might enjoy First Amendment privileges to publish his opinions, but apparently postal officials thought it acceptable to use their government power to punish him for those beliefs.

Fortunately, Suarez's description of federal courts ultimately proved wrong in his own case. One judge refused to hear the case. Another told the Postal Service to work out a consent agreement with Suarez and return his mail to him. But the Postal Service apparently continues to seek ways to punish Suarez for his opinions and for beating it in court. In July 1995 a meeting was held between postal officials and representatives from the Federal Bureau of Investigation, Internal Revenue Service, Secret Service, Federal Trade Commission, and Justice Department Criminal Division, among others, concerning future proceedings against Suarez.

There is reason to suspect that such abuses could increase in the future. Whenever government power is mixed with free institutions, the free institutions suffer. For example, printed material such as books and newspapers enjoy First Amendment free-speech protections. So do telephone conversations. Unfortunately, television and radio broadcasts are subject to censorship.

With the telecommunications revolution the distinctions among the media are breaking down. It is possible to read a book, newspaper, or other material on a computer screen hooked up to the Internet, or to have conversations via keyboards. But in the Telecommunications Act of 1996, the U.S. Congress expanded censorship to the Internet. Specifically, the law makes it a crime to knowingly display indecent or patently offensive material to children under 18, a broad and vague standard that now will cover a wide range of content that is permitted not only in print but even on cable television.

The more the Postal Service attempts to integrate its activities with those of the private sector or with electronic forms of communications, the greater the danger that it will get its wish from the late 1970s to control e-mail.

Snail Mail or Electronic Future?

Few imagined the spectacular developments in telecommunications over the past two decades. This revolution provides a model of private-sector efficiency and innovation. An entirely new information-processing and communications sector with incredible services has been created by dynamic entrepreneurs. More and more, faxes and e-mail replace letter mail for communications. So far the paperless office has not come about, and the actual volume of mail has continued to increase. Yet integrated, multimedia systems increasingly will be introduced into homes and offices during the next decade, promising new 21st-century services. Those systems will more easily facilitate business communications, which currently constitute over 30 percent of the mail. Customer and consumer bill payments, which constitute 15 percent of mail, more and more will be done electronically. Advertisements, which make up almost half the mail, more and more will be delivered on-line. Even household-to-household personal correspondence, which constitutes only about 8 percent of the mail, will benefit from telecommunications progress. Greeting cards now can be generated and customized by computers. With less-costly, high-quality printers it will be easier to surprise friends and relatives with hard-copy best wishes without resorting to the mail.

It is impossible to predict for certain the evolution of communications over the next two decades or the specific role of mail delivery in the mix. But it is possible to say with certainty that the evolution will be distorted and retarded if the government postal monopoly continues to exist. Suppliers of innovative services always will be slowed by the elements of their services dependent on the Postal Service. They will stumble over postal regulations. They will be blocked by the weight of the costly 800,000 postal employees. They will fight constant battles against Postal Service attempts to extend control over their activities and against unfair government-subsidized competing services.

Abolishing the Last Monopoly

The case for privatizing the Postal Service is clear. Indeed, the burden of proof should be on those who would retain the postal monopoly. The correct question to ask, then, is not "Should the Postal Service be privatized?" Rather, it is "Is there any compelling reason for maintaining the postal monopoly?" The answer is a loud and ringing "No!"

The Postal Service survives through sheer political power, not through its ability to satisfy customers. As the country moves into the 21st century, and as policymakers attempt to restore economic liberty, those policymakers should show the courage to abolish the last monopoly and privatize the U.S. Postal Service.

Notes

1. Quoted in Mark Lewyn, "The Check's Still Not in the Mail," *Business Week* (March 18, 1994), p. 38.

2. Bill McAllister, "Millions of Letters Undelivered," *Washington Post* (July 20, 1994), p. A1.

3. Jonathan Franzen, "Lost in the Mail," *New Yorker* (October 24, 1994), p. 62.

4. Matthew Purdy, "Mystery in the Bronx: Third-Rate Service for First-Class Mail," *New York Times* (March 12, 1994).

5. Quoted in Kenneth J. Cooper and Bill McAllister, "Mail Delays Spur Investigations," *Washington Post* (July 22, 1994), p. A4.

6. Cited in Bill McAllister, "Postal Service Better, Especially in Maryland," *Washington Post* (December 20, 1995), p. A23.

7. Cited in John Merline, "Can the Postal Service Deliver?" *Investors Business Daily* (October 28, 1994), p. 2.

8. Figures compiled by the Center for Responsive Politics in Washington, D.C.

9. Alvin Snyder, "The Post Office Is an Ad Agency's Dream," *San Francisco Chronicle* (March 10, 1994).

10. *Washington Times* (August 10, 1995).

11. U.S. Congress Joint Economic Committee, *The Future of Mail Delivery* (June 18, 1982), p 12.

12. Cited in Nadine Strossen, *Defending Pornography: Free Speech, Sex, and the Fight for Women's Rights* (New York: Scribner, 1995), pp. 226–27.

13. Benjamin D. Suarez, *7 Steps To Freedom II. How to Escape the American Rat Race* (Canton, Ohio: The Hanford Press, 1993), p. A126.

14. *Ibid.*, p. A130.

15. *Ibid.*

PART I

THE STATE OF THE POSTAL SERVICE

1. The View from the U.S. Postal Service

Marvin T. Runyon

I appreciate the opportunity to share my thoughts on the central question: "Is it time to privatize the Postal Service?"

If this were 1975 or even 1985, you would have heard a clear answer from the Postal Service. It would have been a resounding "No!"

I am tempted to give that answer today. But it is not that simple anymore. Times have changed, and the world with them. The U.S. Postal Service must change, too. And we are. In fact, we are leading the change.

We understand that America is rapidly moving to a more information-based, service-oriented economy. And it is vital that we have a low-cost, high-quality postal communications system to support it. As humble and ordinary as the mail may seem, the 580 million letters, bills, packages, advertisements, and publications we carry each day form the backbone of our country's economic and cultural vibrancy. And, as evidenced by the $54 billion our customers will spend on postage this year, America communicates through the mail in a big way.

But we in the Postal Service also see the reality of communications alternatives all around us. Computers and fax machines give us the opportunity to send and receive messages within minutes. Home shopping channels, 800 numbers, and interactive TV allow us to order tickets, clothing, and merchandise with the push of a button. Meanwhile, private delivery companies have monopolized the delivery of packages and overnight mail. Even the check is not always in the mail anymore. More and more, it is being sent and deposited electronically.

The Postal Service has six major product lines—from advertising mail to parcels. Each is a big business, which, standing alone, would

The author is the U.S. Postmaster General.

be in the Fortune 200. Yet we are losing market share today in four out of these six business categories.

You talk about privatization. Well, we are being "privatized" every day by our competition—letter by letter, package by package. Competition is giving us plenty of incentive to improve. It is making us realize that if we are to be an innovative leader in the communications industry, we have got to get out there and compete for every postal dollar we get.

The only way to do that is to become more like a private company—in effect, to "corporatize" ourselves. And that is exactly what we are doing. When it comes to running a business, I learned a lot in my years at Ford and Nissan. I came to government, first at the Tennessee Valley Authority (TVA) and then to the Postal Service, because I wanted to prove that these same practices could work in the public sector.

They do. TVA is a customer-driven, top-performing organization. It has not had a price increase since 1987 and has pledged to keep prices steady for a full decade, until at least 1997. It is proving that an organization that is part government and part business can be successful and competitive.

The Postal Service is also more businesslike than ever. We got a good start 25 years ago, when the Postal Reorganization Act combined our mission to serve everyone, everywhere, every day, with a mandate to operate like a business. And we have delivered.

We have become more businesslike, as the act envisioned. Political affiliations no longer determine who gets what jobs. Postal management, with help from a board of directors similar to ones in the private sector, determines our strategic directions and capital investments. And we are self-supporting. Today, when it comes to postage rates, what you see is what you get. There is no longer a 25 percent hidden subsidy in the price of a stamp. No tax dollars fill our coffers. And the real price of a stamp when adjusted for inflation is about the same today as it was back in 1971.

Still, the American people expect even more from us. We are a government organization whose customers have private-sector expectations and demands.

We are stepping up to the challenge. For example, we are injecting the best management practices of the private sector at every turn, such as using the Baldrige criteria[1] to assess our operations, the same yardstick used by many private-sector companies to measure true business excellence. We have redirected our marketing function to focus on delivering solutions to customer problems and anticipating what the American people will need in the way of progressive communications products in the 21st century.

We have worked to become more customer-driven. We give our customers a voice in the way we do business. They talk—sometimes loudly—and we listen, through meetings, forums, and customer groups.

Mailers were instrumental, for example, in helping us develop a mail-classification reform case that will go a long way toward making our pricing structure more modern and market-sensitive. And we hold ourselves accountable to the American people by measuring our service independently.

These and other efforts are paying off. Today we deliver twice as much mail as we did 25 years ago. And we do it with only 15 percent more employees.

Financially, we are strong. At the request of our customers, we delivered a record four years of steady rates followed by an increase two points below inflation. It is paying off. Revenues and volume are up, and costs are down. Three-quarters of the way through our 1995 fiscal year, we have a $1.5 billion net income.

At the same time, service is better than ever. The occasional service horror stories may still dominate the headlines, but a large majority of Americans are receiving consistent, reliable service, and they appreciate it. According to independent measurements announced on June 13, 1995, 87 percent of local first-class mail is arriving on time, our highest score in history and two full points better than last quarter. And a recent consumer survey by *U.S. News and World Report* and CNN shows that customer satisfaction is high, with 87 percent of Americans saying they are pleased with their mail service.

Customers around the nation are praising the work we are doing. John Clark, president and CEO of CTC, our largest parcel shipper, says: "The Postal Service is doing a great job of combining price and customer satisfaction and delivering them to the customer." And Reg Brack, chairman of Time Inc., calls the U.S. Postal Service the "largest, most productive, and least expensive postal system in the world."

And yet, customers also agree that it is time to make further changes to strengthen the nation's mail system. They say that the

5

Postal Reorganization Act of 1970 was a successful first step in building a businesslike foundation for the mail. But they recognize that there is still a great deal of inefficiency and inflexibility originating from the laws that govern our operations.

Christopher McCormick, senior vice president of advertising and direct marketing for L.L. Bean, echoes the sentiments of many of those in the mailing industry when he says, "We'd like to see the Postal Service operate more like a business. What's preventing that are some of the regulations . . . stemming from the Postal Reorganization Act." He indicates that if his company had to operate under the same set of laws, it would be "out of business within five years."

The specific problems we face are many, and they have been spelled out by a host of customers and other observers in recent months. The Mailers Council, whose members account for three-quarters of the nation's mail volume, calls our rate-setting process "too constraining, too lengthy, and too costly." Their organization and others say this process does not give us the freedom we need to deliver competitive, market-based pricing.

The Advertising Mail Marketing Association and the Association of American Publishers point out that the way we implement new products is out of step with today's marketplace. The latter organization said that the Postal Service "should have the ability, like other businesses, to test new products and services without being required to go through full-blown adversarial proceedings." In addition, both agree that the Postal Service should have the freedom to enter into service agreements with large-volume mailers.

Murray Comarow, the executive director of the 1968 Kappel Commission and one of the founding fathers of today's more businesslike Postal Service, has said that our collective bargaining process is broken. Mandatory binding arbitration, he says, "has not worked and will not work." He says it forces both sides into extreme positions, virtually ending the negotiations before they begin.

The Direct Marketing Association points to a laundry list of other provisions that, when taken together, represent "substantial restrictions" on the Postal Service. They include the provisions that impede how we manage our own cash flow and investment portfolio, the limitations on contracting for international air service at the lowest rates, and the pay caps for top executives that stifle our ability to attract more talent from the private sector.

6

Our unions and management associations shared their observations on postal reform in oversight testimony in early June of 1995 before the House Subcommittee on the Postal Service. Generally, they agreed that the system of binding arbitration could be improved, favor greater workforce incentives to reward superior performance, and support changes that would enable us to be more competitive.

Clearly, it is time to take the next step in postal reform. As this subject has been discussed around the nation, a broad range of actions has been recommended. They have run the gamut from minor legislative changes to selling off the Postal Service lock, stock, and barrel to a private company.

But there *is* a growing consensus that the answer lies between these two extremes. There is agreement that it is not time to get the *government out of the business* of delivering the mail. It is time to get the Postal Service *into business for the American people* by freeing it to compete.

Recent surveys affirm this point. A recent Louis Harris poll says that competition is good for the Postal Service. However, the survey results found that more than three-quarters of both business executives and consumers feel that, despite some flaws, the Postal Service is "the best way to provide mail delivery for everyone at a reasonable price."

A recent national survey by Opinion Research Corporation also found that the majority of Americans favor government delivery of the mail. Seventy-six percent favored keeping the current organization, but making it more flexible. I have heard the same thing from business customers in a variety of sectors and in meetings with members of Congress and representatives of the administration. America does not want a *different* Postal Service—it wants the one it *has* to be more businesslike and responsive to its needs.

How do we proceed? We must all decide, in concert with our policymakers, the best path to take. It cannot be *my* answer, or for that matter, the Postal Service's. It has to be *the nation's* answer.

But let me tell you where I stand. I believe in competition. It produces value for the customer. It forces an organization to continuously improve its performance—to raise quality, lower costs, introduce new products, and increase customer satisfaction. And it has done that for the Postal Service. We want to compete. Give us the chance and we will deliver!

7

I also believe in universal mail service. It has helped bind our nation together and make it a world leader. The ability to communicate and conduct business by mail no matter who you are or where you live is a cornerstone of our society. America benefits from one national system, backed by the full faith and trust of the United States government.

I believe it is time to find the right amount of deregulation that will let the Postal Service operate like a business and compete on an equal footing with other couriers and alternative communications, while still ensuring service to all Americans. I believe it is time to strike a balance between unbridled competition and regulatory inertia, between profit and public policy.

There is a variety of models available to us, successful public- and private-sector organizations whose business practices we can apply. Overseas there are a number of progressive postal administrations whose entrepreneurial freedoms are paying dividends for their nations. Other models are at work right here, systems that are helping American companies set the standard for global business excellence. Together, we can strike the right balance, and make the nation's mail a standard for excellence, too.

Dick Barton, senior vice president of congressional relations for the Direct Marketing Association, reminded us of the importance of the question we are considering during recent testimony on Capitol Hill. He said, "We are dealing with an institution that touches the lives of every American and is of critical importance to the huge segments of American business. We cannot afford to experiment. We must get it right the first time. We need a universal, reliable, and reasonably priced service without interruption."

I agree. The American people are counting on us. We all have a stake in a viable, successful Postal Service. The Congress and the American people are leading the way in changing government to make it work better for the American people. All of us, working together, can change the Postal Service and unleash the power of the mail. We can make the Postal Service an organization that can deliver value and excellence in the next century.

2. The Postal Monopoly Law: A Historical Perspective

James I. Campbell Jr.

The U.S. Postal Service (USPS) today is one of the largest commercial undertakings in the world. It delivers roughly 40 percent of the world's mail. In 1994 it earned revenues of almost $50 billion out of approximately $80 billion earned by the United States's delivery services sector.

An important ingredient in the commercial success of the Postal Service is the postal monopoly law that, in the U.S. criminal code, states:

> Whoever establishes any private express for the conveyance of *letters or packets*, or in any manner causes or provides for the conveyance of the same by regular trips or at stated periods over any post route which is or may be established by law, . . . shall be fined not more than $500 or imprisoned not more than six months, or both.[1] [emphasis added]

The postal monopoly law also is set out in administrative regulations issued by the U.S. Postal Service. Substantive regulations implementing the postal monopoly take up more than 7,000 words. The definition of the key term *letter* alone extends for about 400 words.[2]

These standard texts, however, fail to convey a sense of the fundamental ambiguities that underlie the postal monopoly law. As statutory text, the postal monopoly probably represents the most ancient legislative language to be found in the U.S. criminal code; current law employs phrases and concepts introduced by the English King

The author is a special counsel for postal affairs at the International Express Carriers Conference. He has served as legal counsel for major international express companies for almost 20 years. Views expressed here are those of the author and do not necessarily reflect the views of his client. This discussion is based on material from a longer monograph by the author. ©James I. Campbell Jr., 1995. All rights reserved.

Charles I in 1635. The ensuing 400 years of amendments and interpretations have left a deposit of myths and assumptions that is routinely, yet erroneously, characterized by one advocate or another to support a particular plan to revise the postal laws. An understanding of the history of the postal monopoly law is necessary to allow one to evaluate claims about the scope and purpose of the postal monopoly.

English Precedents, 1635–1660

Although English kings had maintained a royal post for official correspondence since 1516, it did not carry letters from the public. Those were conveyed by private posts. On July 31, 1635, Charles I ordered that the royal post be opened to private letters and packets, and he forbade private postal services.[3] The order set out postage rates for letters based on distance. A *letter* referred to a single sheet of paper and a *packet* to a bundle of *letters*. But in 1637, the king again closed the royal post to private letters.

In 1654 Oliver Cromwell, then the head of government, prohibited private carriage. His motive was apparently security for his unstable government. The postmaster was instructed to keep careful track of all letters and unfamiliar post riders.[4]

Colonial Postal Monopoly Laws, 1692–1775

Before 1692 there was no regular postal service in the American colonies. From that year a rudimentary service organized under a "patent" (an exclusive license) was issued by the English crown to a court favorite named Thomas Neale,[5] and was accepted by legislation in the colonies of New York, Massachusetts, Pennsylvania, Connecticut, and New Hampshire. Maryland and Virginia refused to recognize Neale's patent.[6]

In 1707, the British government folded Neale's patent into the British Post Office and in 1711 extended the Office's operations to Scotland and the American colonies.

In 1775, distrustful of the British Post Office, the Second Continental Congress established its own post office. After declaring independence, the new government under the Articles of Confederation of 1778 vested the Congress with the "sole and exclusive right . . . [of] establishing and regulating post offices. . . ."[7]

Under the Ordinance of 1782, the monopoly over letters and packets was extended to dispatches, signifying the preoccupation with the recent war; dispatches referred to letters of an official or military nature.[8]

Early Postal Practices

The phrase "sending post or with speed" best characterizes postal service in early America. To "send post" was to transport by means of a series of posts, or relay stations, located every 10 to 15 miles along a "post road." *Horse posts* stabled horses for riders carrying letters between towns. Letters were conveyed either by "through post," that is, by means of a single rider who obtained fresh horses at each station, or by "standing post," that is, by a series of riders, each of whom handed the mail to a subsequent rider at the next station. A *foot post* was similar in concept but relied on walking messengers.

Several attributes characterized early postal service:

- **Speed.** To "send post" was virtually synonymous with to send "with speed" (by prevailing standards). Like the "pony express" in the western United States a century later, postal systems provided express transportation that was more rapid and reliable than possible for freight generally. The hoped-for rate of travel was seven miles an hour in the summer and five in the winter.

- **Intercity transport service.** Postal service was an intercity service. Letters and packets were transported from a public place such as an inn, coffeehouse, or dedicated post office in one town to a similar place in another town.

- **Addressee pays.** Postage was paid not by the sender but by the addressee on collection at the destination post office. There was no local collection or delivery.

The term *letter* originally referred to a message recorded by hand, usually on a single scrap of paper just large enough for the message. Envelopes, a French innovation, were not introduced in the United States until the mid 1800s. For privacy and protection, a letter was folded and sealed with wax. Postage rates varied by the number of sheets of paper sent by post. A correspondence containing a single sheet was called a *single letter*. Two sheets of paper, that is, two *letters* or a *single letter* with an enclosure, such as a deed or certificate, were called a *double letter*. Three sheets constituted a *triple letter*.

As it was difficult to seal more than three sheets of paper, several sheets might be tied with twine in a bundle or *packet*.

Early U.S. Postal Laws: 1792–1845

The U.S. Constitution, in 1789, authorized Congress to establish "Post Offices and post Roads"[9] but, unlike the Articles of Confederation, did not explicitly establish an exclusive monopoly. The first substantive postal law, enacted in 1792, listed post roads to be established, reflecting the traditional concept of postal service as a long-distance transport. It authorized the Postmaster General to enter into contracts for the carriage of "letters, newspapers, and packets" but limited the postal monopoly to "letter or letters, packet or packets, other than newspapers."[10]

A 1794 act also refers to a *packet* weighing up to three pounds. In postal laws generally, *packet* thus was coming to mean a small package that could include letters, newspapers, or other items.

In 1825, Congress enacted the first general postal code, which it amended in 1827. In the 1831 case of *United States v. Chaloner*, a federal court considered the effect of the enlarged definition of the term *packet* on the scope of the postal monopoly.[11] The defendant was accused of transporting a package of "executions" outside the mails. The Court agreed that "executions" were not *letters* but noted that a package of executions could be considered a *packet*, a term often used in the postal laws to refer to any small package. But the Court concluded *packet* as used in the postal monopoly provision must be interpreted to mean a packet of letters. On this basis, the court rendered judgment for the defendant.

Suppression of Private Expresses, 1845

The concept of a postal service as a rapid intercity transport system operating by means of a series of relay stations on post roads remained essentially unchanged from 1635 to 1835. The Industrial Revolution, however, precipitated a "transportation revolution," which fundamentally altered the concept of a post office. The steamboat was introduced in America in 1807 by Robert Fulton, the steam railroad by Peter Cooper in 1830.

As these means of transportation spread, it was possible to transport large numbers of passengers and quantities of freight at the highest speed attainable. The essential characteristic of the preindustrial post office—extraordinarily fast transportation of small quantities of letters and documents—was rendered unnecessary. Any entrepreneur could board a train or steamboat with letters in his baggage and transport them between cities as fast as the post office. In fact, many did so. It was common for newspapers and other businesses to hire private messengers to convey time-sensitive information. In the late 1830s, regular "private express" companies were organized. Private expresses operated first in the Boston area and on the routes between Boston, New York, and Washington.[12]

At first, the Post Office resisted dependence on the railroads. In 1836, it started its own express service, making improved use of stagecoaches and riders. By 1839, however, it was clear that there was no practical alternative to railroads. The Post Office then discontinued its express service and launched prosecutions against private express companies under the traditional postal monopoly laws. But the courts concluded that use of the railroads was not prohibited by a monopoly over the establishment of horse posts and foot posts.[13]

The Post Office then turned to Congress. Postmaster General Wickliffe claimed that the monopoly over the transmission of *packets* already gave the Post Office a monopoly over the carriage of newspapers and miscellaneous printed matter.[14] He urged increased penalties against private express companies and postal control of railroad schedules. Congress responded with the Postal Act of 1845, which extended the postal monopoly to include intercity transport by private express as well as by post. Congress rejected the postmaster general's call for postal control over railroad schedules. Additionally, the 1845 act introduced a separate rate status for circulars and miscellaneous printed matter (there were no mail classes denominated as such).

Congress implicitly rejected the contention of the Postmaster General that the postal monopoly term *packet* already included newspapers and other printed matter. But it also employed new, more inclusive phrases, *mailable matter* and "matter properly transmittable in the United States mail." This referred to all types of written and printed matter, other than bank notes and books, that could then be transported "in the United States mail," including newspapers, magazines, pamphlets, and "all other written or printed matter whereof each copy or number shall not exceed eight ounces in weight."

Postal Acts of 1863 and 1872

Until the Postal Act of 1863, the Post Office remained essentially a contracting office for intercity transportation services.[15] In fiscal 1862, costs of intercity and foreign transportation constituted 63 percent of all expenses.[16] Before 1863, intercity letters were either held at the destination post office for collection or delivered by a "letter carrier" who acted as an independent contractor and charged the addressee two cents, one of which went to the Post Office. A person could drop letters at a post for delivery by a letter carrier within the same city, but that was a secondary service as far as the Post Office was concerned; even after the 1863 act, such "drop letters" were considered "not transmitted in the mails of the United States."[17]

Delivery of local, intracity letters was pioneered by private companies such as Boyd's Despatch in New York City and Blood's Despatch in Philadelphia. One authority has counted 147 private local postal companies.[18] The "locals" introduced adhesive postage stamps at least as early as 1841. The Post Office did not introduce stamps until 1847 and did not require their use until 1851. Efforts by the Post Office to suppress the locals failed when, in 1860, a federal court ruled that the postal monopoly pertained only to the transportation of letters over "post roads" between post offices and did not prohibit the delivery of letters within a single postal district.[19]

The Postal Act of 1863 introduced several major changes. First, it enlarged the mission of the Post Office by providing for "free" city delivery in major cities, that is, delivery without charge to the addressee. Second, it divided the mail into three "classes" and defined letter postage by weight step instead of number of sheets of paper. In this manner, the original meaning of the term *letter* (a single sheet of paper) lost any practical significance.

The Postal Code of 1872[20] extended the postal monopoly to the delivery of local letters, banning intracity private carriers. It also reverted to the phrase *letters and packets* to define the scope of mail within the monopoly, thus eliminating the 1845 phrase "other matter properly transmittable in the United States mail."

By that time, the term *miscellaneous matter* had grown to include a range of articles weighing up to four pounds, including seeds, cuttings, bulbs, roots, and scions.[21] But such mail appears to have been a negligible portion of postal revenues during that period. If the 1872 act had reenacted the 1845 phrase "other matter properly transmittable," the result would have been a monopoly over the carriage of assorted packages weighing up to four pounds, a substantial enlargement of the monopoly.

Reversion to the phrase *letters and packets* in the 1872 act left unclear the status of certain wholly or partially written documents used in commerce and generally referred to as *commercial papers*. They included manuscripts for publication, deeds, transcripts of records, insurance policies, waybills, bills of lading, invoices, and the like.

In 1881 Attorney General Wayne MacVeagh determined that such commercial documents were not within the *letter* monopoly. He stated, "It is prohibited, and an offence, to carry 'letters or packets.' What is a letter I can make no plainer than it is made by the idea which common usage attaches to that term."

Government Monopoly over Railroad Mail

By the 1890s, large railroads were coalescing into great national systems of roads with interlocking directorates and cross stock ownership. Their complex organizations depended on the smooth integration of a host of smaller and simpler companies,[22] and thus they generated a constant flow of documents between companies with closely interrelated activities.

A railroad train typically included not only cars belonging to the railroad company that owned the locomotive and the tracks but also freight cars operated by express companies, freight cars owned by other railroads, and passenger cars operated by companies such as Pullman. A railroad company might operate trains over not only its own tracks but also tracks belonging to other companies. Railroads were also closely integrated with other types of companies. Telegraph companies used railroad rights-of-way for their lines and provided services for both the railroad and general public, often using joint employees and sharing both costs and profits. Similarly, hotels and restaurants were built along railroad rights-of-way and were integrated with, or alternatives to, dining and sleeping car services.

The Post Office had traditionally acquiesced in the railroads' carriage of letters and documents relating to those interrelated operations.[23] But beginning in 1896, the Post Office asserted that a railroad violated the postal monopoly if it transported its own mail to or from other companies,[24] or transported another company's mail in connection with joint services provided with the railroad.[25] Further, the Post Office held that a railroad could not send mail by special messenger over the lines of another railroad.[26]

To apply the new rulings, the Post Office also had to decide whether various documents unique to railroad operations were to be considered *letters and packets*. On January 7, 1897, the assistant attorney general for the Post Office, John L. Thomas, advised that "car tracers" and "junction reports" were *letters*. Those documents were standard forms listing movements of railroad cars; they were completed in writing but unsigned and addressed impersonally to a position such as "car accountant" at a given station. Thomas reasoned that "the omission of the names of the senders and addressee in the reports and tracers does not change their substance and character."

In the same opinion, Thomas held that files of documents relating to "claim papers"—packages of accumulated correspondence and documents sent to various parties in the course of investigating a claim for lost freight or baggage—were not to be considered *letters*. Thomas opined that "a letter which has reached the party for whom it was intended and has served its purpose ceases to be a letter thereafter. . . ."

In applying its monopoly to railroad mail, the Post Office for the first time employed an administrative, abstract definition of the term *letter* not rooted in the original distinction between letters and *commercial papers*. It did not ask whether a particular type of mail was more like the one or the other. Thomas's approach to railroad mail cannot easily be reconciled with the traditional distinctions. His rationale would include within the monopoly documents listed as examples of *commercial papers* in the 1878 Universal Postal Convention that was attempting to establish international postal standards and definitions. Similarly, it is hard to believe that unsigned lists of railroad cars would be deemed *letters* by the test of Attorney General MacVeagh: "the idea which common usage attaches to that term."

The Post Office continued the practice of using a flexible definition of terms such as *letter*, standing alone. For example, in 1901, the second assistant postmaster general cited the 1897 definition as authority for classifying "tissue copies" of waybills as letters,[27] even though waybills were arguably within the traditional concept of *commercial papers*.

Opinions of Solicitor Lamar, 1916

The Post Office extended its monopoly further by a series of opinions written on March 10, 1916, by William H. Lamar, the Post Office Department solicitor. Lamar considered the lawfulness of a messenger system established for the carriage of "fire insurance policies, bills of debits and credits, and other insurance data" between insurance companies, agents, brokers, and a common clearinghouse called the Chicago Board of Underwriters. The clearinghouse and insurance agents were all located within a single office building. Lamar ruled first that the corridors of a public building served by letter carriers were "postal routes."

Concerning whether insurance documents were *letters*, Lamar quoted with approval a dictionary definition ("a written message, usually on paper, folded up and sealed, sent by one person to another") and briefly referred to dissuasions of the term *letter* culled from three federal cases. The first case, dealing with postal fraud, used *letter* in a context wholly different from the postal monopoly.[28] The second case concerned the mailability of obscene *letters*; it not only bore no relation to the postal monopoly but, in fact, had been overruled.[29] The third case was an 1851 Supreme Court opinion holding that an order for goods was "clearly mailable matter" and thus covered by the postal monopoly law of 1845.[30] The principle derived from these sources was that "a letter is an insubstantial message in writing." On this basis, Lamar reasoned that all writings could be deemed *letters* and that therefore the monopoly included all first-class matter.

On October 13, 1916, Lamar also ruled that the postal monopoly prohibited the private carriage of insurance documents transmitted in bulk shipments averaging 12 pounds. He held that such shipments were *letters* because they were being transported "for the purpose of detecting any discrepancies that may exist in rates, form, or details."[31] (In 1918, Lamar held that "carbon copies" of business documents were *letters* and not *commercial papers* if sent "not merely for filing purposes but for [the addressee's] information and perhaps, where necessary, attention."[32]) With these opinions, Lamar articulated a rationale that could be used to claim virtually any written document was a *letter*.

On May 5, 1916, Lamar held that the postal monopoly also forbade a railroad from transporting printed circulars that were being distributed to members of a railroad union. Lamar conceded that circulars were third-class rather than first-class matter, but stated, without legal authority, that "as respects the postal monopoly the term 'letters' has a broader signification and embraces 'circulars.' "

Between June 1921 and November 1951, postal solicitors issued some 166 opinions dealing with the postal monopoly. Most claimed a monopoly over the carriage of various items. Almost all were devoid of legal citations of any sort. Referring to the Chicago Board of Underwriters opinion, one of those opinions sought to include in the definition of the term *letters* "live communications."[33] Another, in 1929, claimed monopoly over the transportation of computer cards, and by implication all computer data.[34]

Notwithstanding the broad rationale advanced by Lamar, the Post Office did not actually try to enforce a monopoly claim over the entirety of either first- or third-class mail. The Post Office continued to recognize that certain types of first-class matter were not included in the *letter* monopoly, for example, checks, insurance policies, legal documents, official records, maps and drawings, newspaper copy, and telegrams.[35] Those were, in fact, vestiges of the commercial papers category of mail. With respect to Lamar's claim of a monopoly over third-class matter, the Post Office Department backed down completely. In 1919, the postmaster general assured a congressman, "This Department has never attempted to assert a monopoly in the carriage of mail matter other than that of the first class included unquestionably in the phrase *letters and packets*.[36]

Speaking more plainly, for example, Postmaster General Walter F. Brown in 1930 testified to Congress, "As you understand, *we have a monopoly only of first-class mail*. That is the trouble. . . . We have a monopoly of only sealed-letter mail. *We have to come into competition with every sort of carrier on everything else. . . .*" [emphasis added].[37]

Today's U.S. Postal Service

The Postal Reorganization Act of 1970 replaced the Post Office Department with the U.S. Postal Service, an independent federal agency. In 1974, the Postal Service adopted comprehensive monopoly regulations that substantially revised the previous administrative definition of *letter* to read "a message in or on a physical object sent to a specific address."[38] This definition manifestly included within the postal monopoly all physical communications, whether recorded by means of writing, printing, photography, or electromagnetic process. In response to criticism that the proposed definition of *letter* incorrectly covered *commercial papers*, long held outside the monopoly, the Postal Service referred vaguely to the authority of "original general definitions":

> [Checks and other commercial papers] were declared not to be letters on the theory that they are evidence of rights of the holder rather than written messages. Such a theory is inconsistent with the *original general definitions of "letter"* because such documents are in fact messages, conveying information of several kinds [emphasis added].[39]

Similarly, the Postal Service responded to objections to the inclusion of newspapers in the definition of *letter* by explaining:

> Newspapers and periodicals also meet the tests in *past guidelines* for determining what are letters . . . [an] exclusion of newspapers and periodicals seems of doubtful validity. [emphasis added].[40]

To mitigate opposition to its new definition of *letter*, the Postal Service also issued regulations that purported to "suspend" the postal monopoly, creating administrative exceptions for newspapers, magazines, checks (when sent between banks), data processing materials (under certain circumstances), urgent letters, and international remail.[41] While the suspensions have prevented politically powerful mailers from petitioning for congressional review of the postal monopoly, as a matter of law, Congress never authorized the Postal Service to suspend the postal monopoly. As statutory authority for the suspensions, the Postal Service cites an 1864 Postal Act.[42] However, it is apparent from even a superficial reading of the legislative history of the act[43] that this provision was never intended to confer authority to suspend the postal monopoly. The gist of the 1864 law was to allow the postmaster general to reapply the postal monopoly by suspending, on a selective basis, an exception to the postal monopoly allowing private carriage of letters in stamped envelopes.

In applying its new definition of *letter*, between 1974 and 1978, the Postal Service's lawyers advised mailers that the monopoly included the carriage of items such as payroll checks, Walt Disney posters, fishing licenses, professional football tickets, IBM cards, blueprints, data processing tapes and computer programs, gasoline company credit cards, intracompany memoranda, and documents that are electronically transmitted and converted to hard copy form, when being carried from the telecommunications receiver to the addressee or from the sender to the telecommunications transmitter.[44]

The only major federal case to consider the meaning of the terms *letters* and *packets* since 1970, indeed since 1872, was *Associated Third Class Mail Users v. U.S. Postal Service.*[45] Decided in 1979, a divided D.C. Circuit Court of Appeals held that printed advertisements were within the postal monopoly over *letters* and *packets*. The court's judgment was based substantially on the 1974 Postal Service regulations and the 1916 railroad circular opinion of Solicitor Lamar. Although the case relied heavily on historical analysis, the court was plainly uninformed about several key elements of the history of the postal monopoly law, including the 1881 opinion by Attorney General MacVeagh and the 1919 letter to Congress (drafted by Lamar) disclaiming a monopoly over first-class mail.

Conclusion

The postal monopoly law of the United States is derived directly from a temporary decree issued by Charles I in 1635. It was last debated by Congress in 1845. The statutory precedents from this preindustrial period depend on concepts of *postal service*, *letter*, and *packet* that are so old and foreign to the modern world that the very meanings of words have changed. Nonetheless, building upon these legislative precedents, Congress enacted the current postal monopoly law in 1872, introducing unexplained revisions, apparently as a result of suggestions by the Post Office in 1863, when it first began delivery of mail to a small portion of the U.S. population.

After enactment of the 1872 act, the scope of the postal monopoly depended on the validity of various *administrative* definitions promulgated by the Post Office Department and, after 1970, by the Postal Service. Immediately after enactment of the 1872 act, it was generally held that the scope of the monopoly depended on the definition of the term *letters* (a *packet* being accepted as a letter of several sheets). Following a ruling by the attorney general in 1881, the Post Office considered that the *letter* monopoly included only first-class items that could not be described as *commercial papers*. Subsequently, the administrative definition of *letter* was enlarged in three major steps: in the mid 1890s, while the Post Office was dueling with the railroads over the right to carry "railroad mail"; in 1916, when a Post Office lawyer made broad claims based on questionable legal bases; and in 1974, when the Postal Service issued the first comprehensive postal monopoly regulations.

In interpreting the statutory and administrative provisions setting out the postal monopoly today, recent Supreme Court cases leave little doubt that history matters.[46] The light of history, however, makes clear that the facile assumptions about the scope and purpose of the postal monopoly law must be viewed with extreme caution.

Notes

1. 18 USC 1696(a).

2. 39 CFR 310, 320. The definition of "letter" is found at 39 CFR 310.1(a).(1)-(a)(6).

3. Proclamation of July 31, 1635, Patent Roll (Chancery) 11 Car. I, Pt. 30, No. 11.

4. See generally, II. Robinson, *The British Post Office: A History*, (1948; reprint, Westport, Connecticut: Greenwood Press, 1970), pp. 48–55.

5. Post Office Act of 1660, 12 Charles II, c. 35 (1660).

6. W. E. Fuller, *The American Mail: Enlarger of the Common Life*, (1972; reprint, Chicago: Chicago University Press, 1980), pp. 18–19.

7. Articles of Confederation, Art. IX.

8. Ordinance of October 18, 1782, 23 J. Cont. Cong. 670.

9. Art. I, sec. 8.

10. Act of February 20, 1792, ch. 7, §14, 1 Stat. 232, 236.

11. *United States v. Chaloner*, 25 F. 392 (D. Maine, 1831).

12. See George Rogers Taylor, *The Transportation Revolution*, 1815–1860 (1951; reprint, New York: Rinehart, 1951). The classic history of the rise of the express companies is A. Harlow, *Old Waybills* (1934; reprint, New York: Arno Press, 1976).

13. See, for example, *United States v. Thompson*, 28 F.Cas. 97 (D. Mass. 1846); *United States v. Adams*, 24 F.Cas. 761 (S.D.N.Y. Nov. 1844); *United States v. Kimball*, 26 F.Cas. 732 (D. Mass. April 1844).

14. *Report of the Postmaster General in relation to the establishment of a private express between New York and New Orleans*, S. Doc. No. 66, 28th Cong., 2d Sess., at 3 (Jan. 21, 1845). In arguing that *packet* was used broadly in the postal monopoly provision, Wickliffe was probably relying on an 1843 opinion by Attorney General Nelson that declared, without referring to the *Chaloner* case, that the term *packet* included "newspapers, magazines, or pamphlets " 4 Ops AG 276 (1843).

15. Act of March 3, 1863, ch. 71, 12 Stat. 701.

16. *Annual Report of the Postmaster General (1862)*, p. 190.

17. Act of March 3, 1863, ch. 71, §23, 12 Stat. 701, 705.

18. E. Perry, *Byways of Philately*, 1 (Federalsburg, Maryland: Mrs. H.W.K. Hale, 1966).

19. *United States v. Kochersperger*, 26 F.Cas. 803 (E.D. Pa. 1860).

20. Act of June 8, 1872, ch. 335, 17 Stat 283.

21. Act of March 3, 1863, ch. 71, §20, 12 Stat. 701, 705.

22. A. Chandler, *The Visible Hand*, (Cambridge, Mass.: Belknap Press, 1977), pp. 171–87.

23. 3 Ops Sol POD 140 (Op. No. 1111) (June 26, 1896) (acknowledging practice of allowing railroads to carry railroad mail); Postmaster General Order No. 422 (July 2, 1896) (declares monopoly will be "rigidly enforced" against railroads).

24. 3 AAG POD 132 (Op. No. 1107) (June 3, 1895); 3 AAG POD 140 (Op. No. 1111) (June 26, 1896).

25. 2 AAG POD 877 (Op. No. 956) (1890) (telegraph); 3 AAG POD 140 (Op. No. 1111) (1896) (hotel).

26. 3 AAG POD 146 (1896).

27. Letter from the second assistant postmaster general to J. D. B. DeBox, assistant general counsel, Nashville, Chattanooga & St. Louis Ry, dated July 13, 1901.

28. *United States v. Denicke*, 35 F.407 (C.C.S.D. Ga., 1888).

29. *United States v. Gaylord*, 17 F.438 (C.C. S.D. Ill., 1883) considered whether an obscene "letter" was within the scope of a postal law provision that made obscene "writings" nonmailable. *Gaylord* held that a "letter" is a "writing" within the context of the law. The Supreme Court disagreed in *United States v. Chase*, 135 U.S. 255 (1890).

30. In *United States v. Bromley*, 53 U.S. (12 How.) 88 (1851).

31. 6 Ops Sol POD 457 (1916).

32. 6 Ops Sol POD 606 (1918).

33. 7 Ops Sol POD 131 (1921).

34. 7 Ops Sol POD 699 (1929).

35. See, for example, Post Office Department, *Restrictions on Transportation of Letters*, 5th ed. (1967) pp. 9–14.

36. Letter from Acting Postmaster General J. C. Koons to Halver Steenerson, chairman, House Comm. on Post Office and Post Roads, dated August 18, 1919.

37. Hearings on H.R. 14246, the Post Office Appropriation Bill for 1932, before a Subcomm. of the House Comm. on Appropriations, 71st Cong., 3d Sess., at 227–28, 230 (1930) (emphasis added).

38. 38 Fed. Reg. 17513 (1973) (proposed §310.1(a)). The key terms of the definition were in turn defined.

39. 38 Fed. Reg. at 17513.

40. 39 Fed. Reg. at 3969.

41. See 39 CFR 310.1(a)(7) n. 1; 39 CFR 320.

42. Act of March 25, 1864, ch. 40, 13 Stat 37, codified at 39 USC 601(b).

43. See *Cong. Globe*, 38th Cong., 1st Sess., 1243 (1864).

44. See PES Letter 74-24 (1974) and PES Letter 75-1 (1975); PES Letter 75-5 (1975); PES Letter 76-5 (1976); PES Letter 75-32 (1975); PES Letter 75-11 (1975); PES Letter 74-14 (1974); PES Letter 78-11 (1978); PES Letter 76-8 (1976); PES Letter 74-7 (1974) and PES Letter 74-15 (1974); and PES Letter 78-14 (1978), respectively.

45. *Associated Third Class Mail Users v. U.S. Postal Service*, 440 F.Supp. 1211 (D.D.C. 1977), *aff'd* 600 F.2d 824 (1979), *cert. den.* 444 U.S. 837 (1979).

46. *Regents of Univ. Cal. v. Public Empl. Rel. Bd.*, 485 U.S. 589 (1988) (scope of the "private hands" exception to the postal monopoly); *Air Courier Conference of America v. American Postal Workers Union*, 498 U.S. 517 (1991) (rejecting standing of postal union to enforce the postal monopoly).

3. Postal Service Problems: The Need to Free the Mails

Peter J. Ferrara

Any analysis of the U.S. Postal Service must begin with this basic fact—it is the classic economic definition of a monopoly. It is not just a big company with lots of market power. It is an actual government-granted, government-protected, government-mandated legal monopoly. A citizen competing in the delivery of addressed first- or third-class mail will be subject to prosecution under federal criminal law, and subject to imprisonment. The robber barons never had it so good.

High Costs, Low Quality

The most basic economic analysis leads to the conclusion that such a legal monopoly will produce some combination of higher prices, lower supply, and lower quality. Why? Because a legal monopoly is not restrained by competition or subject to incentives to perform well. All up and down the chain of command, the organization is not subject to the daily pressure to keep costs down and quality up. Its managers do not enjoy the freedom of their private-sector counterparts to pressure workers to maximize output and minimize waste and cost. Its managers cannot easily be dismissed for poor performance. A government monopoly need not produce the best service for consumers, in contrast to organizations that must meet competition every day. Its leadership is not looking out for the latest cost saving or quality-enhancing innovation. It need not be concerned about those matters because its customers are captive by law. They cannot turn to a competitor with lower prices or higher quality, or who has adopted the latest innovations first.

The author is the chief economist and general counsel at Americans for Tax Reform. He is the editor of the book *Free the Mail: Ending the Postal Monopoly*, published by the Cato Institute.

Indeed, without the restraint of competition, the legal monopoly can abuse the public for its own gain. Even a nonprofit monopoly like the Postal Service can overpay its bureaucracy in salary, perks, and benefits, and send the bill to the customers. It can also ease the work obligations on its employees, allowing them to take it easy.

This is not just theory. These have been the actual results of monopolies in the real world over and over again. And that is exactly the result one would see with the Postal Service.

The 1995 New Year was greeted by a 10 percent increase in stamp prices, to 32 cents. That is up from 8 cents in 1971. But inflation is not the benchmark. In telecommunications and other areas subject to modern technological innovation there has been a rapid decline in prices over the period. But not in the Postal Service. Despite the expenditures of billions of dollars in automation by the Postal Service there has been no perceptible impact in reducing total costs. Indeed, worker productivity seems to have fallen during that time.[1]

Indeed, I submit that the Postal Service's fees are double what they would be in a free market. Consider the evidence:

- In a recent study published by the *Journal of Regulatory Economics*, Thomas Lenard estimates that third-class mailers pay $2.5 billion per year in excess, unnecessary costs to the Postal Service. This is almost one-third of their total postal service fees.[2]
- A broad review of the economic literature by Robert W. Hahn and John A. Hird concluded that the postal monopoly increased costs to consumers overall by between $4 billion and $12 billion per year.[3]
- The Postal Service's own internal studies show that costs for rural routes on which services are contracted out to the private sector are about 50 percent less than the cost for the Postal Service to provide the same service directly.[4]
- Private letter-sorting bureaus presort mail for the Postal Service for less than half of what the Postal Service cites as its own costs of doing the same work.[5]

When the opportunities for complementary services and revenues discussed below are considered as well, one can see how postal rates in a competitive free market could well be 50 percent less than they are today.

Yet, while postal prices have risen over the past decades, postal service quality has not kept pace. In 1969, for example, a first-class letter took on average 1.50 days to reach its destination. By 1987 it took on average 1.72 days.[6] Mail delivery overall was 15 percent slower than 20 years before. That is truly remarkable. In what other area of communication can such deterioration be found?

Further, the Postal Service's system for measuring mail delivery speed counts only the time from when the letter leaves the originating post office to when it arrives at the final postal facility, not to when it is actually delivered to the customer. In addition, the Postal Service is notorious for seriously fudging even those numbers. As James Bovard reports:

> A 1987 Postal Inspection Service survey, for example, found widespread cheating by local post offices. Cleveland clerks told inspectors of 'subtle forms of intimidation' from management to get good results. As *Business Mailers Review* noted, "Two postmasters, in a candid moment, said that if [on-time delivery] tests were conducted by private auditors, the percentage of letters reported to be delivered on time would drop by as much as 20 points." Employees are "under substantial pressure to come up with right numbers," and some have been bumped out of their jobs because they refused to cheat on the mail delivery tests.[7]

In the late 1980s, the Postal Service came up with another way essentially to cheat on the numbers. In scores of cities across the country, including the major metropolitan areas, it moved up the final mail pickup time each day to 4 p.m. from 5 p.m. or later. So everything dropped off after 4 p.m. would be counted as having been dropped off the next day.

Service has declined in other ways as well. Years ago, the Postal Service delivered twice a day to the doorstep of each home. That service was cut back to once a day. Then service began to move from a mailbox at the door to a mailbox at the street. Lately, the Postal Service has been promoting the use of so-called cluster boxes at a central site for each neighborhood, where the customer would have to go each day to pick up the mail. As one postmaster told a reporter, "The old days of mail being taken to your home are coming to an end."[8] Remarkably, the Postal Service seeks to retain the monopoly but no longer to provide the service.

In the past the Postal Service has had serious problems with mail that is lost, or even junked by carriers. Undelivered mail has been found in recent years piled up in the back of trucks, stashed in back yards, or even buried in shallow, unmarked graves. Bovard writes,

> For example, a Rhode Island carrier was arrested after 94,000 letters were found buried in his backyard. A 1987 survey by Doubleday and Company found that up to 14 percent of bulk business mail was thrown away or lost. One Arlington, Virginia, postal clerk told a customer, "We don't have room for the junk mail—so we've been throwing it out." In 1987, 1,315 postal workers were fired for theft or mistreatment of mail, or both. A Postal Inspection Service audit found properly addressed mail dumped in the trash at 76 percent of the post offices it visited.[9]

In some urban areas, in fact, mail delivery has recently all but collapsed, with haphazard deliveries, nondelivery for extended periods, and routine loss of mail. Chicago is the clearest example of this situation, where residents have lost magazine subscriptions, insurance coverage, and credit cards because they could not reliably get the payments through by mail.

All this should come as no surprise. The Postal Service is quite literally an enterprise run on the old Soviet economic model—a monopoly government bureaucracy. Now the current postmaster general, Marvin T. Runyon, can try to succeed where Mikhail Gorbachev failed if he wants. He can try to reform the state monopoly to make it work. But Gorbachev was at least as smart as Runyon and he could not do it even with the KGB. Indeed, no one has ever done it. Analysis says it cannot be done.

No Public Policy Rationale

In most other areas of the economy government monopolies do not exist and antitrust laws purport to prohibit private monopolies, though these latter cannot exist without government collusion. Yet the federal government mandates a postal monopoly. That makes no sense. There is no sound public policy rationale for the postal monopoly.

The federal postal system was started to ensure some reliable means of communication with the far-flung frontiers of Indiana and Kentucky in an age when hay-eating, flesh-and-blood horses carrying quill-penned messages on parchment paper constituted the national communications network. Today, by contrast, the entire country is thoroughly wired for communication—by telephones, television, radio, faxes, cable, satellites, computers, e-mail, and the Internet. Reliable communications between New York and Montana pose no problem. Indeed, a number of private firms such as Federal Express, Guaranteed Overnight Delivery, and United Parcel Service deliver packages and overnight letters anywhere in the nation.

In this context, mail delivery is not a unique or critical service. It is just another business that can and should be done through the competitive private market.

The official argument for the postal monopoly is that the mail is a natural monopoly. The mail can be delivered most efficiently and at lowest cost by a single nationwide firm, the argument goes. But the rationale could not be more illogical. The correct policy response for a natural monopoly is rate regulations to prevent excessive prices and profits, not a law prohibiting competition. Granting a legal monopoly to a supposed natural monopoly would be unnecessary at best, and at worst counterproductively self-fulfilling in precluding competition that could otherwise arise.

Moreover, the markets for package delivery and overnight mail show that the mail is not a natural monopoly. Several firms compete for both package and overnight mail delivery.

Another rationale advanced for retaining the postal monopoly is that it is necessary to ensure universal service throughout the country. Postal Service supporters claim that private firms would deliver only to the lower-cost, more profitable areas. They would allegedly skip areas where mail delivery is more costly, such as rural areas where greater distances between homes would increase costs.

But this argument seems insupportable in light of current market performance in other areas. It is the free market that guarantees universal service, not the government, and not the postal monopoly. Everywhere and anywhere there is a demand for a service, the market provides it. What good or service is not available in rural America today? The private market delivers food, clothing, shelter, medicine, video games, beer, guns, computers, TV sets, even illegal drugs to rural America. The idea that it cannot deliver the mail seems nonsensical given the reality for other goods and services.

Further, the private package delivery firms and private overnight mail firms in fact deliver to rural America and the entire country. They already provide universal service, without a government

27

monopoly. They do so because of the pressure of competition. Customers do not want to waste time going to an office to send a package or letter if there is a chance they may be told that the company does not deliver where they want. So private firms are forced by the market to offer universal service to satisfy consumers.

Former Federal Trade Commission chairman James Miller ultimately called the bluff of the Postal Service on the question of rural mail delivery. He suggested that the postal monopoly be removed only in the rural areas that the Postal Service claims private competitors would not serve. The proposition could then be fully tested. The Postal Service declined the suggestion. That shows the Postal Service does not believe its own rhetoric on this issue.

The private market may deliver to rural areas, a critic might concede, but at what price? The best answer might be about half of what the Postal Service charges today, based on the analysis above. The inefficiencies of the status quo postal monopoly overwhelm the true costs of rural postal delivery.

But, a critic might ask, would a uniform national rate be retained in a private system? The answer is, such rates should not necessarily be retained. If the real cost of sending a letter from Miami to Seattle is higher than the cost of mail delivered from one Miami address to another, customers should pay the costs of the services they consume. If an uneconomical uniform rate is retained, the below-real-cost prices for those in some areas mean above-real-cost prices for those in others.

But the experience in the private market again is not only universal service but primarily universal, uniform rates. The private package delivery services and overnight mail firms generally charge uniform national rates without geographic distinctions. They do so because they have found the real cost differences to not be worth the complications and administrative costs of varying rates. There may also be marketing efficiencies in being able to advertise a single national price. When a uniform national price is most efficient and meets consumer demand, that is the right market price.

Finally, the question of universal service and uniform rates has nothing to do with a postal monopoly. If the public thinks that mail should be delivered to every address and at a flat rate, the government can adopt regulations requiring all private mail delivery firms to provide such services and rates as they compete against the

Postal Service. That result can ultimately be mandated without a postal monopoly. The above discussion, however, shows such regulation is unnecessary. It would indeed only counterproductively preclude market alternatives and innovations the public may ultimately prefer.

The experience in mail delivery categories where the monopoly has already been removed suggests what would happen if competition for first- and third-class mail were allowed. For delivery of packages and overnight mail, the private competitive market works quite well. In each case, several firms rigorously compete in providing high-quality universal service at reasonable cost-based prices. Indeed, the private competitive market works so well in those areas that the public has overwhelmingly favored the private market over the Postal Service. The public has given more than 90 percent of its business in those two areas to the private competitive market, and less than 10 percent to the Postal Service. That is quite damning and definitive. It is far more compelling than any poll. When people are free to choose in the real world, they choose freedom over bureaucracy. This experience demonstrates that the public would favor repeal of the postal monopoly and freedom to participate in the free market.

Free the Mail

Postmaster General Runyon sees the handwriting on the wall. His policy pronouncements indicate that he is more interested in being Boris Yeltsin than Gorbachev on the postal monopoly. He has stated in recent speeches that the status quo is not viable for the Postal Service. It cannot function under the current restrictive environment of political control. It cannot design and bring new services to market in the current web of government regulation. In fact, he has said that an individual can conceive and bring a new child into the world faster than the Postal Service can bring a new or changed service to the market.

Runyon has also complained that regulations prohibit price flexibility and that too strict regulation of Postal Service financing prevents the new investment needed for innovation. He has also complained of excessive political control over property, post offices, and labor relations. Runyon is seeking to free the Postal Service of those restrictions. But it will never be freed of such political control as long as it is a government monopoly. There is no way a government bureaucracy and a monopoly will be allowed to choose its own products and services, and investments and financing, free of political control. There is no way a legal monopoly can be given pricing flexibility. As long as the Postal Service is a government monopoly, politics and not economics will dictate its labor relations, its post office locations, and its use of property.

But Runyon's concerns suggest the private sector solution to the Postal Service's problems. It would include the following:

- The Postal Service would be given the free-market flexibility Runyon wants, with removal of the restrictions described earlier.
- Ownership of the Postal Service would be moved to the private sector by issuing stock, with some if not all ownership granted to the employees, as Reps. Phil Crane and Dana Rohrabacher have suggested.
- In return, the Postal Service's monopoly would be removed, allowing all private sector competitors.

How would such reforms work? They would work much like the current private markets for packages and overnight mail delivery. Several firms would compete nationwide for mail delivery, providing universal service at universal rates. Rates would be sharply lower than current Postal Service charges for monopolized first- and third-class mail, perhaps 50 percent less. Yet service would be vastly improved, with much greater reliability and speed. The public would be satisfied with the market's performance, as it is today for packages and overnight mail delivery.

But the Postal Service itself would be remarkably transformed. Subject to competition and market incentives, it would slash costs, and greatly improve quality, to market levels. The problem with the current system is not the people employed at the Postal Service, but the institutional arrangement and incentives under which they must operate. With full market incentives, they will be able to perform at world-class standards.

Indeed, the new Postal Service will probably be the largest private mail delivery firm by far. Without a guaranteed market that it could retreat to, it probably would charge back into package and overnight mail delivery in a rigorous and highly competitive way, winning substantial market share. But it probably would go well beyond that, exploiting its comparative advantages.

One of those advantages is that the Postal Service is the largest landlord in the United States, with 40,000 properties nationwide.[10] With new market incentives, the Postal Service likely would move vigorously to put the properties to best use. Some of the properties can be sold at great profit, having been purchased for relatively little many years ago. Others can be rented out for maximum use. But probably the greatest potential is to rent out space in every postal facility to complementary vendors—selling packaging and envelopes, copying services, printing, faxes, even letter stuffing. This would all greatly increase the Postal Service cash flow.

But even beyond this, the new free-market Postal Service is likely to move aggressively into offering complementary services directly. The close complementary nature of the services with the postal business offers great profit potential. At the same time, consumers would enjoy great convenience and cost saving.

And this does not even begin to explore what complementary services can be offered on the delivery side of the business. What else can mail carriers do while they are delivering the mail? Can they deliver other goods and services? Can they carry advertising on their trucks? Can the stamps carry advertising messages?

Indeed, in that market environment, postal service is likely to see innovations we do not even yet imagine. Only a decentralized competitive market offers the full opportunity for those with local practical knowledge to experiment and bring forth the winners.

Those wide-ranging opportunities for the new Postal Service are the factors that suggest that postal rates in a free market would be even lower than studies currently indicate. At the same time, the new free-market Postal Service would be a large, highly profitable, world-class firm. The employees who would share in its ownership would benefit greatly from this. The value of their shares would probably be far greater than the currently estimated $30,000 per employee. Business mailers would benefit greatly as well. They would be able to deal with a depoliticized commercial entity, as in all other areas of their business, rather than a political bureaucracy. As a result, they would get much better service at much lower cost. The same benefits would result for average consumers.

Indeed, there is no alternative to this course. Current policies are a death sentence for the Postal Service. Without change, virtually all business-to-business communication will shift to electronics rather than suffer under the government monopoly status quo. This is in fact well under way. Just over the horizon, businesses will require electronic payment of bills by consumers, through home computers and interactive home video as well as through automatic teller machines, rather than allowing unreliable, slow payment through government monopoly mail bureaucracy. The majority of the Postal Service's current business will then be gone, leaving an inadequate volume base to support its current organizational structure and employee base. The system will then collapse, putting current direct mailers out of business and leaving only an electronic communications alternative for them.

The only viable alternative is to do the right thing—free the mail.

Notes

1. See speech by Postal Rate Commissioner Patti Birge Tyson at the Direct Marketing Association, Washington, D.C., May 15, 1987.

2. Thomas M. Lenard, "The Efficiency Costs of the Postal Monopoly: The Case of Third-Class Mail," *Journal of Regulatory Economics*, 1994, 421–32.

3. Robert W. Hahn and John A. Hird, "The Costs and Benefits of Regulation: Review and Synthesis," *Yale Journal on Regulation*, vol. 8: 233 (1990): 264.

4. Peter J. Ferrara, *Free the Mail: Ending the Postal Monopoly* (Washington, D.C.: Cato Institute, 1990), p. 2.

5. Ibid, p. 19.

6. *Origin-Destination Quarterly Statistics Report, FY 1988, Quarter 1*, U.S. Postal Service, p. 7.

7. James Bovard, "The Slow Death of the U.S. Postal Service," in *Free the Mail*, p. 15.

8. Ibid, p. 19.

9. Ibid, p. 13.

10. See Advertising Mail Marketing Association, "Putting Postal Assets to Work," Washington, D.C., January 1995.

4. Mass Mailer Problems

Gene Del Polito

From a business mailer's perspective, four key things are needed from a postal system. (1) The system must have the ability to deliver mail anywhere in the nation; (2) it must provide services that are timely and reliable; (3) it must facilitate communication and commerce; and (4) it must render services at prices the market is willing to pay. From the advertiser's perspective, today's postal system fails to satisfy those very basic business communication needs, and there is little likelihood that the U.S. Postal Service (USPS)—as it is constituted today—will have any hope of fully satisfying those needs tomorrow.

Over the past two years the USPS made headlines in newspapers around the country when problems affecting mail service in Chicago and Washington came to light. Postmaster General Marvin T. Runyon was criticized severely in the press and on Capitol Hill as critics set out to take a pound of flesh from his hide. The postmaster, never one to duck an issue, took the criticisms in stride and promised to take immediate and effective action to improve mail service in Chicago, Washington, or anywhere else that needed attention.

By mid 1995 Runyon and his senior management team were taking delight in announcing that mail delivery service was showing signs of significant improvement in key metropolitan areas around the country, and that mail delivery performance was now the best since the Postal Service starting measuring it through an outside auditing service. Does this mean the days of crisis are over? Is everything fixed? Have the Cassandras been put in their place? Is the Postal Service really a rising phoenix?

As a matter of fact, the Postal Service is still a sick institution, as virtually nothing has been done to rectify the cause of its ills. Let

The author is the executive director of the Advertising Mail Marketing Association.

33

me try to put matters in a different perspective with an analogy that, while strong, is illustrative nonetheless.

The Depth of the Disease

The USPS as it is constituted today can be likened to a human infected with an immune deficiency. Immunodeficiency is an insidious disease. Unless it is detected early through a serum analysis, it does not show its ugly head until it has degraded a person's immune system sufficiently to allow other diseases to appear that ordinarily would not affect humans with healthy immune systems. Those diseases are described as "opportunistic," because they show up only when an immune system deficiency provides an opportunity for them to flourish.

Opportunistic illnesses can be treated. In fact, in most persons with advanced immunodeficiency disease, physicians try to keep the opportunistic ills under control through aggressive treatment. It is not uncommon to see infected individuals respond to such treatment. In fact, if the treatment is on-target and aggressive enough, the patient's health can appear to improve measurably. Indeed, it is not uncommon for some infected individuals to believe that somehow they are "over the hump," when aggressive therapy provides them symptomatic relief.

Are they "over the hump?" Unfortunately not. That is the really insidious part of the immunodeficiency disease. In fact, the symptomatic relief is at best temporary, because virtually nothing has been done to purge the person of the immunodeficiency infection that gave opportunistic illnesses the chance to rear their ugly heads. As long as the virus remains, the patient is still in danger; and, if an effective treatment is not applied, the patient's immune system will continue to degrade to the point at which the disease becomes incompatible with life.

Analogously, in spite of the promising news the USPS has recently been able to share, virtually nothing has been done to purge this patient of its immunodeficiency-like disease. In fact, what postal officials have done to date is to treat as aggressively as they can such opportunistic infections as "Chicago" and "Washington." Millions of dollars have been spent on technological and human resources to straighten out a mail delivery system gone awry.

34

As one would expect, such aggressive treatment has had some positive effect. Indeed, it would have been surprising if it had not. The patient is experiencing symptomatic relief, but until something is done to purge the USPS of its peculiar disease, its prognosis remains poor. Consider the evidence of its precarious state of health.

Falling Postal Business, Electronic Competition

The postmaster general himself has acknowledged that the USPS's share of its "first-class mail," predominantly business-to-business financial transactions, market has eroded by a third over the past five years and will erode by yet another third over the next five. The telephone, fax machine, electronic mail, electronic data interchange, and electronic funds transfer are used in lieu of mail by more and more businesses across the United States.

That is a serious matter, because this business previously would have taken the form of first-class mail—a product line that provides the USPS with 61 percent of its operating revenue. Postal officials are mindful of this, but they evince a false sense of comfort in some recent growth in business-to-household and household-to-business mail—even though there are readily apparent signs that even this mail is not immune to electronic diversion.

The number of homes with facsimile machines and fax-modem-equipped computers has grown phenomenally. Automated teller machines are everywhere, and consumers have become more comfortable using the machines, "smart phones," and personal computers for most of their day-to-day financial affairs.

Twenty years ago, home shopping television did not exist. Today it does. Cable now brings dozens of channels into businesses and homes across America. Cable broadcasting's diverse programming has segmented a mass audience in a way many advertisers and marketers find desirable. The same sort of audience segmentation is occurring with radio broadcasting as well. Today, programming that is designed to appeal to audiences with remarkably different tastes allows advertisers and marketers to find in the conventional media ready outlets for their targeted messages.

The Internet no longer is the plaything of academics and scientists. It is rapidly becoming a vehicle for everyday communication and commerce. The World Wide Web has made libraries of information and entertainment available to everyone, and cybermalls, once only

35

a concept, now are a reality. While only a gleam in some visionary's eye 10 years ago, few now doubt that within the next decade interactive TV will transform the way Americans get their information and entertainment and communicate with each other. Clearly, no mail market is safe from electronic diversion, and it would be sheer folly to disregard the financial consequences of any such changes on our postal system. The postal patient is not on the road to recovery, because the root cause of its ills remains untreated.

Sources of Sickness

Ironically, the genesis of the Postal Service's ills can be found in the very act by which it was created, when Congress restructured the Post Office Department into today's USPS. While that law did many things, it failed to change the fundamental institutional character of the Postal Service. It is today what it always has been—an agency of government directed by law to operate on a cost-plus, no-profit basis driven by cultural imperatives that are antithetical to success in a contested market.

Former postmaster general Anthony Frank perhaps described that culture best, when he noted that under today's contractual rules, when a productive city letter carrier completes his appointed rounds in less than the contractually allotted time, the consequence for the carrier is more work. The consequence that awaits the goldbricker, on the other hand, is overtime with extra pay. When the rewards say "shirk" rather than "work," the credo is not "no risk-no gain," but rather "no gain, so why risk."

The concepts of cost-minimization and profit-maximization have no meaning in a world where the only statutory imperative is to raise prices if costs increase. Congress may never have intended the USPS to be a competitive enterprise, but to thrive, let alone to survive, the Postal Service must find its way amid intense marketplace competition. Doing that requires an ability to adjust quickly to changing marketplace needs and conditions—a characteristic the Postal Service sorely lacks because of its present legislative and regulatory structure.

This USPS is a tightly regulated entity because it has a statutory monopoly over the carriage of letter mail. New communications technologies, however, have eroded much of the buffering the monopoly status once provided, and rate regulation has exacted from the Postal Service a very high price.

While others can introduce new products and services in the market at will, the Postal Service must petition the Postal Rate Commission for permission to introduce innovations. While others can adjust their prices and position their products in the market virtually at will, to attain the same ends, the USPS must undergo an expensive and contentious regulatory process—one that typically is used by its competitors to deny the USPS unfettered access to the marketplace. In addition, as a government agency, the USPS is constrained in other matters that are key to the conduct of its affairs.

Reality in one respect is as Marvin Runyon has portrayed it. The nation's postal legislative and regulatory framework is an anachronism. The world that existed when Congress enacted postal reorganization no longer exists today, and the legislative and regulatory constraints under which the Postal Service must function make it absolutely impossible for it to adapt quickly and effectively to changing marketplace realities and demands.

This situation must change, because the reality that must be faced is that while the role mail plays in the nation's communication and information infrastructure is changing, the need for a universal mail delivery system will not diminish—at least not for the foreseeable future. Whether the services are rendered by something called the "U.S. Postal Service" is a matter of less importance than having access to mail services that facilitate, rather than impede, commerce and communication. The challenge, then, is to determine how better to provide for the nation's needs in a rapidly changing world.

Curing the System

The American people have a long and abiding commitment to free enterprise and competition. It has been a hallmark of American domestic and international policies and has served as a bulwark in the struggle against imperial communism. It remains today a defining character of the United States's continuing efforts to advance human rights and democracy in an uncertain world, and it is long past time that the commitment to free enterprise and competition be brought to the nation's postal system.

Congress has a myriad of alternatives from which it can provide for the nation's postal needs in the decades ahead. It could opt, for instance, to leave things as they are and address the matter of taxpayer subsidies for the USPS when the need finally arises. Alternatively, it could hang the "For Sale" sign on the government post office and sell off the enterprise in whole or in parts. It also could choose among several other alternatives that lie somewhere in between the extremes of the polar opposites of subsidy or privatization.

The Good Book cautions against putting new wine in old skins, and my mother once told me that one cannot make a silk purse out of a sow's ear. Similarly, I can see no way of purging the USPS of the root cause of its ills without transforming it from the protected enterprise it is today into a more private-sector-like, market-driven, competitive enterprise.

One way to do that might be to reconstitute the USPS along the lines of other government-sponsored enterprises such as Fannie Mae, Freddie Mac, or COMSAT. This is a model that has been used for postal systems elsewhere in the world, and it certainly might be suitable here. Gaining the kinds of market and regulatory freedoms the postmaster general says he would like to enjoy, however, would require the USPS ultimately to give up its monopoly. Without the monopoly, there would be no need for regulation to serve as a proxy for competition, as competition would exist in ample measure in the marketplace.

As a government-sponsored enterprise, the Postal Service could be transformed into a true stock corporation. Government, then, could have the option to be the enterprise's sole stockholder, its majority stockholder, or its largest single minority stockholder. Under such a model, the USPS would be charged with operating on a truly commercial basis, that is, at a profit, paying taxes, with stock dividends, and subject to antitrust and all other such laws that apply to commercial enterprises.

As a stockholder, the federal government could require a regular and substantial preferred rate dividend that could be used to help reduce the nation's deficit and debt. The nation, then, could benefit from its two centuries of investment in the postal infrastructure in a way that would be impossible under today's framework. The federal government also could choose to make stock available to the enterprise's employees through an employee stock ownership plan or some other form.

Employee ownership, in whatever measure, could foster a very different relationship than presently exists between the USPS and its workers. Postal employees, from management on down, would have a personal and vital stake in ensuring the ability of the enterprise to thrive—and not just survive—in a changing and competitive market. The new stake could help lessen the tension and acrimony that often have characterized labor-management relationships.

As a commercial, competitive enterprise, a postal corporation that is chartered as a government-sponsored enterprise would be expected to conduct its financial affairs in accord with sound private-sector corporate practice. It would be free to establish banking relationships that best suited its needs, and it would be free to borrow in the public markets—with or without the federal government as a guarantor. Postal employee organizations could expand their stake in and strongly affirm their commitment to the Postal Service's marketplace success and well-being by investing employee retirement funds in postal corporate obligations that could be used to provide for the enterprise's capital needs.

Once the constraints imposed by third-party regulation are removed, the USPS would have the freedom to conduct its affairs in the same manner as other commercial enterprises. It could organize and position its services in whatever manner best met marketplace needs. It could price its products in closer accord with market-based principles. It could innovate freely and introduce to the market new products and services that made good business sense. It could explore entry into new markets without undue regulatory constraints, and it could exit markets as long as doing so did not compromise its statutorily defined mission. It also could be freed from constraints that are more in keeping with agencies of government, such as the present limits governing the compensation of its executive staff and its Board of Governors.

Accomplishing this sort of major transformation cannot be done precipitously. An orderly transition would need to be provided to ensure a smooth glide path from the postal system that exists today to that which ideally should exist tomorrow. Such a transition might entail a phased elimination of the letter-mail monopoly over time with commensurate reductions in regulatory constraints.

Particular attention would need to be given to rules that would open the postal system to competition to ensure that mail service remains universal in reach, rendered in a cost-efficient and reliable manner. No one, not even the USPS's present or prospective competitors, would benefit from a collapse of the nation's postal system, and every effort would have to be made to ensure against such a catastrophe.

The proposal outlined here is far from complete. A great many details would require Congress's attention to ensure that the federal government's and the Postal Service's rightful obligations to all postal employees are suitably honored. It also should be recognized that what is proposed here represents only one of any number of alternatives from which Congress could choose. Indeed, other designs, once examined in detail, may prove to be preferable.

In the long run, the form any future postal system takes is of less importance than the manner in which it functions. The paramount concern of all mailers is that there will be, for as long as the nation needs it, a postal system that can provide timely, reliable, affordable, and universal mail delivery.

Diagnosing an ill is often easier than implementing an effective cure. What is offered here is a beginning. Now the hard work must be done.

PART II

COMPETING WITH THE POSTAL SERVICE

5. Competing Carriers

Thomas M. Lenard

The U.S. Postal Service (USPS) provides a traditional industrial age service—the delivery of messages in hard-copy form. The USPS is being challenged by a variety of new, Information Age communications alternatives. The alternatives already have eroded the Postal Service's share of the communications market, and will continue to do so in the years ahead. However, a mail-delivery service will remain an important part of our nation's communications and information infrastructure well into the 21st century.

The erosion of the Postal Service's core business leaves customers increasingly finding themselves contending with rising rates and inadequate services. The situation will only worsen as new technologies eat into the Postal Service's markets and undermine its financial viability. To cover costs, the Postal Service will be forced to raise rates to levels normally unsustainable in the marketplace. These circumstances will impose hardships on those who, because of the letter mail monopoly, have no viable hard-copy message delivery alternative, and on the taxpayers, who ultimately may be forced to subsidize, through their tax dollars, a growing and costly postal infrastructure.

The Postal Service's status as a government-owned monopoly makes it virtually impossible for either the Service or its customers to adapt to rapidly changing technology. It is therefore imperative to seek to replace the way the United States's postal services are structured. The form the replacement will take is far from straightforward; imaginative solutions that accommodate the competing interests that have a stake in the current framework need to be developed.

The author is director of regulatory studies and a senior fellow at the Progress and Freedom Foundation in Washington, D.C.

Competition for the Postal Service

As a government-owned enterprise protected from competition in the major markets in which it operates, the Postal Service occupies a unique place in the American economy. The Private Express Statutes give the Postal Service a monopoly over the carriage of "letter mail," which covers all first-class and most third-class mail. Together, those two classes make up over 80 percent of the Postal Service's business.

The principal argument against permitting competition in the delivery of mail is that the Postal Service is a natural monopoly, able to provide mail services at a lower cost than if it shared the market with other firms. The contention that the Postal Service is in fact a technological natural monopoly has not been, and probably will not soon be, econometrically resolved. Potential economies of scale and scope notwithstanding, private firms can effectively compete with the Postal Service, when permitted. United Parcel Service (UPS) and Federal Express are well-known success stories. The fact that the Postal Service faces as much competition as it does, in both service quality and price, from a variety of sources, despite its statutory monopoly, is indicative of the high cost of maintaining the status quo.

The Efficiency of Public Firms

The evidence that costs tend to be inflated in public enterprises relative to their privately owned counterparts is overwhelming. In general, public firms have higher costs and prices, faster rates of price increase, higher and more rapidly increasing wages and salaries per unit of output, and more slowly increasing productivity levels than private firms in comparable industries.[1]

A major reason for the inferior performance of public firms with respect to various efficiency indexes is the diffuseness and nontransferability of ownership that characterize those enterprises.[2] While the separation of ownership and control can and does create problems for private firms, the "agency" problems are much more severe for public enterprises.

The fact that ownership shares in private companies are transferable fosters efficiency in a number of ways, not the least of which is that the impact of management decisions is visible in the value of the company's shares. Inefficiencies and inflated costs are likely to be reflected in a decline in share price. One consequence of this may be an increased threat of takeover by those who may be able to correct management failures. Even in the absence of a takeover threat, however, managers have a strong incentive to see that the company is run efficiently. There is substantial evidence that managerial remuneration in private firms is closely tied to the performance of the company's stock.

None of those incentives is present in public enterprises. The owners of a public company (i.e., the taxpayers) are not able to divest themselves of their shares in the company; thus incentives for management to detect and correct mismanagement are far weaker than in a private company. Moreover, the fact that the implications of management decisions are not capitalized into the value of the firm's outstanding shares may lead public managers to focus too much on short-run business strategies. Thus, public firms are frequently biased toward the use of labor (or other variable inputs) and away from capital investment.[3]

Importantly, the empirical evidence suggests that competition improves the cost-efficiency of public enterprises, even if they may still suffer in comparison with privately owned and operated firms.[4] Thus, far from increasing costs to consumers, permitting competition in the provision of public services is likely to lower costs and result in consumer savings.

Private Carrier Cost Comparisons

Recently, the argument has been advanced that, even if the Postal Service exhibits constant returns to scale in its transportation and sortation functions, it is likely that there are substantial scale economies associated with local delivery.[5]

Analysis of data from small private delivery firms suggests that that is not the case in any meaningful sense.[6] Many technologies have engineering economies of scale and scope, but few industries are considered natural monopolies. A large-scale operation might manifest managerial diseconomies and bureaucratic inefficiencies that may outweigh the advantages of purely engineering economies. There is no benefit to mailers in being forced to rely on a high-cost provider of a service, even if those high costs are to some extent mitigated by the presence of scale or scope economies.

While it is clear that large firms such as UPS, Federal Express, and others are strong competitors, there is also evidence concerning the viability of smaller enterprises that deliver advertising and promotional mail. The evidence comes from survey data my colleagues, Monica Bettendorf and Stephen McGonegal, and I gathered and used to analyze the cost structure of the small, private mail-carrier industry that operates today, subject to the constraints of the letter-mail monopoly. The small, private carriers deliver unaddressed advertising mail and, to a lesser extent, periodicals and catalogs that may be addressed.

Note that, in the context of the letter monopoly, the term "addressed" connotes something different from whether a piece of mail physically carries an address. All Postal Service mail is required to carry a written address, even if it is delivered to all addresses in an area. In the context of this analysis, the term "addressed" refers to mail that is targeted or selectively delivered and therefore is covered by the postal monopoly. Advertising circulars that are delivered to most or all of the addresses in an area, that is, are not selectively delivered, are considered unaddressed, and therefore may legally be delivered by private firms. Periodicals—second-class mail—and most books and catalogs also fall outside the definition of letter mail and may be privately delivered.

The private-carrier data we used were obtained from mail survey responses from a sample of private mail carriers in 1989. The firms varied considerably in size, but none had annual revenues in excess of $20 million and the majority had annual revenues below $2 million.

One of the interesting things we found was that the small firms that make up the private mail delivery industry have been offering a variety of mail preparation and other services in connection with the basic delivery service, many of which are not offered by the Postal Service. For example, private carriers offer

- selective targeted coverage based on various demographic characteristics;
- guaranteed delivery on a specific day;
- coordination with printers; and
- Sunday and holiday delivery service.

None of these services is offered by the Postal Service.

The survey questionnaire we submitted to the small firms contained sets of questions on addressed and unaddressed delivery operations and sought job-specific data on up to 10 recent delivery jobs for each firm. We obtained data on the prices and service characteristics of 117 of the jobs. We used the data to estimate the private-sector costs of providing third-class delivery services.

Using data from the private mail delivery jobs, we estimated a private mail-carrier cost function. We then compared private-sector carrier costs with USPS third-class bulk rates. The principal purpose of estimating the cost function was to determine the additional cost associated with delivering addressed mail. We then used the cost differential to convert the unaddressed rates from the private job sample to addressed rates to better reflect the actual USPS third-class mailstream, which consists primarily of addressed mail. To compare the private rate structure with the USPS rate structure, we computed a USPS rate for each of the jobs in the private-carrier sample, using the USPS schedule of discounts for presorting, drop-shipping, and/or automating mail. The results show the following:

- Not surprisingly, there are some economies of scale in the private mail delivery sector. The cost of delivering a piece of mail is inversely related to the density of the route, as measured by deliveries per mile. That is to say, the denser the population, the lower the costs per piece delivered. There are also economies associated with delivering a number of pieces together, rather than delivering each piece individually.
- Economies of scale notwithstanding, the stand-alone costs of providing private bulk advertising mail service were significantly below the Postal Service's third-class bulk regular rates. The private rate was below the Postal Service rate for 80 percent of the jobs in our sample, and the average private rate was 73 percent of the USPS rate. The results are only partly attributable to the Postal Service wage premium. A substantial amount of the excess Postal Service costs are not explained by higher labor costs.

The stand-alone cost test is designed to ensure that purchasers of regulated goods and services are not paying supracompetitive prices. Clearly, the Postal Service has not been passing this test.

The extent to which the sample of private mail delivery jobs that we used is representative of private-sector delivery costs is difficult to determine. There is, however, no reason to believe the sample is seriously flawed. Despite clear differences between the Postal Service and the small private carriers from which we obtained data, they do provide very similar services:

- First, they deliver a broad array of promotional materials.
- Second, they provide a variety of sortation and other services, including services not provided by the Postal Service.
- Third, they deliver to a mix of high- and low-density regions, indicating that private firms do not achieve viability simply by "cream-skimming." Delivery jobs in isolated areas, such as Alaska, Montana, and Idaho, were not represented in the sample, but those areas do not account for a significant portion of the Postal Service's business, either.

It is important to emphasize that the data do not come from the UPSs and Federal Expresses of the world. They come from small mom-and-pop operations. To the extent that economies of scale and scope are important in that market, the Postal Service should enjoy advantages that are unavailable to the private carriers—especially the small firms that operate there. The fact that they can compete suggests either higher costs or mispricing on the part of the Postal Service.

What do the private carrier cost estimates imply for the aggregate costs of the letter monopoly? Third-class bulk regular rate mail accounts for $8.3 billion, or about 18 percent of the Postal Service's business. The cost data we collected suggest that almost one-third of that amount—about $2.5 billion—represents excess costs to mailers attributable to the postal monopoly.[7]

The excess costs paid by mailers represent some combination of transfers between groups and efficiency costs, which represent a pure loss to the economy. Since the Postal Service does not yield any return to the Treasury, and is, in fact, required by statute to break even, it can be concluded that monopoly rents are not being earned by the owners of the Postal Service—that is, the taxpayers. There is, however, substantial evidence that postal labor benefits from the postal monopoly. In what is probably the most widely cited study on the subject, Jeffrey M. Perloff and Michael L. Wachter found that postal workers were paid a premium of 21 percent relative to their private-sector counterparts.

Using that estimate, and assuming that the transfer is borne disproportionately by users of first- and third-class monopolized mail, implies that at least $1 billion of the $2.5 billion higher cost represents efficiency costs, with the remainder consisting of transfers to postal labor. That postal labor is a major—perhaps the major—beneficiary of the postal monopoly is well understood and is important when it comes to developing reform proposals.

The Postal Service's first-class business, all of which is protected from competition by the letter-mail monopoly, is more than three times as large as its third-class business. Caution should be exercised in extrapolating the third-class results to the first-class monopoly. The private mail carriers whose cost data were used to generate the third-class efficiency costs provide a service directly comparable to USPS third-class mail delivery. The extent to which this service is comparable to first-class delivery is less clear. Nevertheless, the results are indicative of the general magnitude of the costs to the economy and to mailers.

Since the time our survey was taken, the private delivery sector has grown substantially:

- Private delivery services are now offered by more than 38 percent of the daily newspapers that responded to a 1994 survey by the Newspaper Association of America.[8]
- Five years after Publishers Express was founded in 1989 by Time Inc., it delivered about 60 million magazines and catalogs and about 6 million "ride-alongs."[9]
- About 70 percent of the nation's 100 million households now are covered by private mail delivery of some kind, according to a 1994 survey by the industry publication *Optimum Delivery*.[10]

Nevertheless, the extent to which private delivery can penetrate the market is obviously limited—by the letter monopoly and by the letter-box restrictions.

Competition from Electronic Transmission

In the long run, the Postal Service is probably more vulnerable to competition from electronic forms of transmission,[11] which can completely bypass the existing legal restrictions. Electronic competition has been foreseen for years and is not new, but its intensity is growing. There are, for example, now at least 9 million installed fax machines and increasing use of computer-generated fax transmissions. A 1994 General Accounting Office (GAO) report found that e-mail was growing at 25 to 30 percent per year. The market for on-line services is expanding as well, with companies like Prodigy, CompuServe, and America Online providing home shopping, banking, e-mail, and a variety of interactive information services.

With respect to commercial transactions, GAO recently found that transfers of data between businesses using electronic data interchange have been experiencing a 30 to 40 percent growth rate. Electronic funds transfer also has been growing rapidly, with more than 35 million invoices paid electronically in 1993.

In 1992, the dollar volume of electronic alternatives to postal delivery was estimated at $47.3 billion—$10.1 billion in messages and transactions, $24.7 billion in advertising, and $12.5 billion in publications. While the Postal Service has not lost business in absolute terms, its estimated share of the market for correspondence and transactions has declined dramatically—from 77 percent in 1988 to 54 percent in 1994.

Those changes are driven primarily by technological advances in computing and telecommunications. The advent of digital transmission technologies is resulting in vast improvements in and increased demand for all forms of electronic communication. Many of the new means of transmitting, storing, and processing data offer the prospect of substantial savings to businesses and benefits to consumers.

There is little the Postal Service can do to forestall the new technologies. Certainly, there is no evidence that their adoption is sensitive to small variations in the Postal Service's rate schedule, as some have suggested. It is, however, important that the Postal Service have the ability to respond and adapt to new circumstances, which it is unable to do operating as a rate-regulated statutory monopoly. Otherwise, the service will represent an increasing financial burden on those of its customers who have limited alternatives, and on the taxpayer.

Redesigning the Postal Service

Given the interests of current stockholders—the taxpayers—how can the system be redesigned? The most obvious group with a stake in the current system is postal labor, but there are others as well, including the Postal Service's competitors, and individuals and businesses in high-cost service areas who fear they will be disadvantaged by a more competitive system.

Americans have always put a premium on the ability to choose. This is apparent in the changes taking place in the telecommunications industries, where choice is facilitated in long-distance service and where a similar system is emerging for local and cable TV.

A plan to redesign the Postal Service should (1) provide the flexibility for the Postal Service to survive and for customers to have a sufficient array of service alternatives, and (2) avoid the service disruptions and taxpayer bailout that might occur if nothing is done. A plan that meets the objectives should be based on the following premises:

- Abolish the government's monopoly over the carriage and delivery of mail. There is no benefit to mailers when they are forced to rely on a high-cost provider of service. The monopoly deprives mailers of needed alternatives, and the USPS itself of the freedom and flexibility to meet mail service and communications needs.
- Remove explicit or implicit special advantages for the Postal Service relative to its private competitors. The Postal Service should be able to compete in new markets on a level playing field.
- Make ownership shares transferable in a new Postal Service. This type of organization promotes efficiency. The government could, however, retain a partial ownership share.

Conclusion

The empirical evidence from the small private distributors of advertising and promotional mail is clear: where competition is allowed to operate, costs are lower, and customers are satisfied. While first-rate overnight and package delivery by large operations such as Federal Express, Guaranteed Overnight Delivery, and UPS are usually cited as examples of how competition works, the same situation is found with smaller operations.

This evidence further undercuts the argument that a government postal service with monopoly powers is needed and strengthens the case for privatization.

Notes

1. See *Annual Report of the Council of Economic Advisers* (1986).
2. See W. Mark Crain and Asghar Zardkoohi, "A Test of the Property-Rights Theory of the Firm: Water Utilities in the United States." *Journal of Law and Economics* 21 (October 1979); David G. Davies, "The Efficiency of Public Versus Private Firms, The Case of Australia's Two Airlines." *Journal of Law and Economics* (1971) 14: 149–65; and Richard J. Zeckhauser and Murray Horn, "The Control and Performance of State-Owned Enterprises," in *Privatization and State-Owned Enterprises: Lessons from the United States, Great Britain and Canada*, ed. Paul W. MacAvoy, W.T. Stanbury, George Yarrow, and Richard Zeckhauser (Boston: Kluwer Academic Publishers, 1989), pp. 7–57.
3. See Crain and Zardkoohi.
4. See Zeckhauser and Horn.
5. See John C. Panzar, "The Economics of Mail Delivery," in *Governing the Postal Service*, ed. J. Gregory Sidak (Washington: AEI Press, 1994) for a discussion of this line of argument. This would mean that an efficient postal system should charge efficient access prices to the local delivery network.
6. See Thomas M. Lenard, Monica M. Bettendorf, and Stephen McGonegal, "Stand-Alone Cots, Ramsey Prices, and Postal Rates," *Journal of Regulatory Economics*, 1992, pp. 243–62.
7. See Thomas M. Lenard, "The Efficiency Costs of the Postal Monopoly: The Case of Third-Class Mail," *Journal of Regulatory Economics*, 1994, pp. 421–32.
8. *Circulation Update*, Newspaper Association of America, March 1995.
9. Advertising Mail Marketing Association Postal Issues Summary, April 1995.
10. *Optimum Delivery*, Willow Bend Communications, December 1994. This figure refers to private delivery of magazines, catalogs, advertising circulars, and other similar items. Federal Express, UPS, and other private companies deliver to 100 percent of the country.
11. Much of this section is drawn from Daniel F. Spulber, Rebuttal Testimony, Postal Rate Commission Docket No. R94-1, September 7, 1994.

References

Thomas M. Lenard, "Comments," in *Regulation and the Nature of Postal Delivery Services*, ed. Michael A. Crew and Paul R. Kleindorfer (Boston: Kluwer Academic Publishers 1993), pp. 128–32.

Jeffrey M. Perloff, and Michael L. Wachter, "Wage Comparability in the U.S. Postal Service," *Industrial and Labor Relations Review*, 1984, pp. 26–35.

Jeffrey M. Perloff, and Michael L. Wachter, "A Comparative Analysis of Wage Premiums and Industrial Relations in the British Post Office and the United States Postal Service," in *Competition and Innovation in Postal Services*, ed. Michael A. Crew and Paul R. Kleindorfer (Boston: Kluwer Academic Publishers, 1991).

6. E-mail, Faxes, and Personal Computers: Telecommmunications Alternatives

Stephen L. Gibson

There Is No "Place" in Cyberspace

The Information Age is upon us, bringing a depth of technological, economic, and societal change not seen since Gutenberg's invention of the printing press and the Industrial Revolution it helped to spawn. Human society is reorganizing itself around knowledge rather than materials, and the implications for information-handling businesses, of which the U.S. Postal Service (USPS) is one, are profound.

It is not sufficient simply to examine the U.S. Postal Service, its structure, operations, and management, and make pronouncements on what changes, including privatization, would make it more efficient. Any discussion of postal operations must place them in the proper context, a context of rapid technological change. Without the broader view, we remain like the natives who discover a car in the jungle: amazed at its wondrous features and creature comforts but, lacking roads, blinded to its true use. In this sense, the debate over postal privatization has broadened beyond the traditional confines of "natural" monopoly, competition, and universal service.

The assorted telecom alternatives such as e-mail, faxes, and personal computers are both actors and playwrights in this ongoing drama, at the same time reflecting and causing changes in the way coded information of all types is handled. And changes are not simply the result of the specific capacities of e-mail or faxes, the Internet or celluar phones. The interplay of all these technologies, and the way they seed further change in every aspect of economic life, is what makes the dynamic new Information Age.

The author is executive director of the Bionomics Institute in San Rafael, California.

53

Traditional models of analysis, based on yesterday's physical organization of society, are inadequate for understanding today's microprocessed virtual reality. The USPS is, above all, about places and things. From its early history, when communication was slow and uncertain, through the development of the railroads, and into the late 20th century, the Postal Service's government-defined niche has been transporting papers and packages from one box to another.

It must be remembered that the Postal Service grew out of a time when communication was difficult at best. As Daniel Roper, the first assistant postmaster general, put it in a 1917 book, "With the population of the thirteen states extending into the vast inland territory, which the national safety required should be held against all European nations, it was imperative that the outlying settlements should be kept in touch with the Atlantic seaboard."[1] There was a very real need for communication, *any* communication, in large parts of the country. That communication was between places.

The very term "post office" reflects this focus on a fixed physical location where one could go to post a letter. When Roper, in his book, devotes an entire chapter to "The Post-Office Lobby," he writes about a "room or corridor for the free use and convenience of the people" and not, as we might expect today, about interest groups seeking special political favors.

More significantly, today's postal operations grew hand in hand with the highest expression of centralized, Machine Age thinking, the railroad. From 1864 to 1917, as railroad lines used by the Post Office exploded from 22,000 miles to 234,000 miles, the number of postal employees grew from 572 to over 18,000.

The Information Revolution

The force that would change information processing and transmission, and thus the conditions in which the Postal Service operates, was born in 1971. That year, just two years after a man landed on the moon, Federico Faggin and his colleagues in what soon would become Silicon Valley invented the microprocessor, or computer on a chip.

Again here, a dose of historical context is illuminating. Some 400 years earlier, Gutenberg invented movable type. Within 40 years, the new printing technology had cut the cost of copying written information a thousandfold. That development, more than any other, stimulated the development of scientific knowledge and, ultimately, led to the Industrial Revolution.

By contrast, in the first 25 years after the invention of the microprocessor, the cost of copying written or any kind of coded information has dropped 10 *millionfold*. Like the printing press, the microprocessor will take us from one age to another. Thus the technological jump-shift that brings the Information Age is already of a magnitude 10,000 times greater than Gutenberg's. And information costs continue to drop.

As microprocessor capacity developed through the 1970s and early 1980s, only minimal effects outside the purview of specialized computer users were evident. Then, about 15 years after the computer chip's invention, societywide effects emerged. Almost overnight, technologies that had been bubbling along for a decade or more seemed to explode. Fax machines, Internet nodes, cellular telephones, e-mail, and countless other microprocessor-enabled communication technologies took off.

The growth rates of the new technologies, like those of processing capacity, are difficult to fathom. Internet host sites are increasing at a rate of 20 percent every three months, a pace sufficient to wire the entire world by sometime near the turn of the century. During the next decade, computing power is expected to rise a hundredfold and "bandwidth," the size of the pipe that digital information, such as e-mail, flows through, is expected to increase a thousandfold. Current fiber optic laboratory research suggests that up to a trillion bits per second will be possible in the future. That speed would allow transmission of every issue of the *Wall Street Journal* ever printed in one second. At that rate a million channels of TV could be sent over one fiber optic strand. And if more capacity is needed, other strands could be added. After all, fiber optic strands, not much larger than a human hair, are made of sand. And those strands, including the switching devices at either end, already are cheaper than copper.

Twenty thousand desktop video units with cameras that allow visual communications were in use in 1994, with a projected 7 million units by the end of 1996. Flash chips, an alternative method of data storage, are forecast by Dataquest Inc. to grow from 250,000 units shipped in 1994 to 8 million by 1998. Digital cash, traceless person-to-person value exchanges over the Internet, may be workable today, and certainly will be tomorrow. Perhaps Mark Rosenker, vice president of public affairs for the Electronic Industries Association, summed it up best when he said, "The business is smoking."

In sum, we are well on our way to a radically different, information-based economy. While we can only guess at its ultimate shape, some clues have emerged. As Nicholas Negroponte put it in *Being Digital*:

> The agent of change will be the Internet, both literally and as a model or metaphor. The Internet is interesting not only as a massive and pervasive global network but also as an example of something that has evolved with no apparent designer in charge, keeping its shape very much like the formation of a flock of ducks. Nobody is the boss, and all the pieces are so far scaling admirably.[2]

Mail: Electronic vs. Paper

To understand the implications of the current information revolution, it is necessary to move away from the existing bricks-and-mortar, paper-and-boxes paradigm that defines communications via conventional mail, and start thinking in terms of an evolving web of information technology. E-mail, for example, is sent to a *virtual*, not a real, address. One does not know where it is going when one sends it. And, at the same time, one can be anywhere and still read it. Indeed, the technology exists today to check e-mail from an airplane, or a moving car, or a mountaintop, or even from the podium while delivering a presentation to a conference on the Postal Service. The Olivetti Company is developing a system that, through a badge, can track where individuals are in a building and make the nearest phone ring.

In sharp contrast to the USPS, electronic communication is erasing the very concept of place. Indeed, the virtual world is one not bounded by traditional anchors; time and space are different, if not absent altogether, in a world of instantaneous global communication. The Information Age economy is an increasingly seamless web of overlapping communication technologies.

Unlike the USPS's world of paper and mailboxes, Information Age communication is between people, not places.

In the early days of postal delivery, it could take weeks to find out about wars, elections, or other national or world events. Today the contrast was seen, for example, when on October 3, 1993, at

11:20 p.m., CNN's Jonathan Mann announced, "The attack on the Russian Legislature is about to begin, and we'll have that for you right after this commercial."

What does instantaneous communication mean for the Postal Service's business of delivering paper messages? Letter writing, like e-mail, is asynchronous. That is, communicating parties do not interact in real time, at the same time, as in a phone call or an Internet Relay Chat. But e-mail is delivered instantaneously and responses can be made as soon as the receiving party reads the message. It is unclear how the tradeoff between paper mail and e-mail will evolve. Telephone calls took the place of many letters, but not all of them. Both burgeoning voice mail and video mail may replace more. Today the country is 60 percent wired for transmission of digital data over traditional telephone lines, which can carry video mail. The country will be 90 percent wired by the end of 1996. But whether that enabling technology will make the video phone calls finally catch on is unclear.

One effect of the information revolution is on the competitive landscape in which the USPS operates. Communications technology is evolving quickly, and the process is accelerating. That the role of traditional paper-based, place-to-place communication will change dramatically is certain. Whether the need for the USPS to engage in mass paper transport will continue to exist is the 800,000-employee question. Would horse-drawn carriages still be built if that business had been a government monopoly at the time when the suppliers of automobile were attempting to find a mass market for their products?

Already, estimates are that 50 percent of calls to and from the United States across the Atlantic and 30 percent of American calls over the Pacific are via fax. Gallup surveys suggest that faxes are 40 percent of telephone charges at Fortune 500 firms. But both the rapid growth rates and the fact that faxes can substitute for either voice calls or letters make true comparison with mail problematic. Fax penetration of businesses has mushroomed from 3 percent in 1985, to 48 percent in 1990, to about 97 percent last year. And telecommuting, possible only with a relatively paperless office, is growing perhaps 15 percent per year.

Less tangibly but still significantly, the availability of inexpensive information fundamentally alters the way information is disseminated. Today's centralized, mass broadcast of advertising, news, and other information with passive consumers on the receiving end will give way to greater consumer selection, with so-called "pull-through" information flows. Consumers will be able to pick and choose, filtering out unwanted information. Tolerance for unsolicited bulk-mail advertising, for example, may decline dramatically. Similarly, the need for paper catalogs likely will continue to diminish as more current, customized, useful information is available on-line. For a similar effect to be seen in first-class mail, all that is needed is the inevitable, if slow-in-coming, shift to paperless offices.

The Internet provides a good example of the rapidly evolving information system that contrasts dramatically with the slow-moving changes at the USPS. With the early Internet, the relatively obscure, hard-to-use UNIX applications of e-mail and file retrieval were the only user-assistance products available. Then Marc Andreesen, a young graduate student, introduced a program called Mosaic that allowed users to browse graphically an interlinked network of host sites known as the World Wide Web. Within about a year, the *de facto* standard Mosaic has been supplanted by a newer, faster product called Netscape. Today, Sun Microsystems has released yet another generation of Web browser. Whether their animation- and multimedia-capable HotJava will become king of the World Wide Web hill remains to be seen.

Even by Information Age standards, the growth of the World Wide Web is astounding. According to "The Internet Index," the number of commercial Web sites increased by 7 percent in one week in June 1995. And more money was invested in Internet companies by venture capitalists in the first quarter of 1995 than in all of 1994. As the chairman of Chrysler Corporation put it, "The large won't eat the small. The swift will eat the slow. Speed is everything."

At the USPS, a simple price change takes 10 months or more.

Expected Pace of Change

All organizations must learn to adapt, as institutions, to technological, economic, and social changes if they are to survive in a dynamic market environment. Early on, the Post Office learned as well. During the fiscal year ended June 30, 1887, just under 1 billion pieces of mail were sorted for delivery on railway mail cars, with error rates of .04 percent. By 1917, 14 billion pieces of mail were sorted with error rates as low as .02 percent, or one error for each 6,366 pieces.

By the mid 20th century, though, the inevitable effects of monopoly—that is, protection from market competition—had taken hold. In recent decades, the inflation-adjusted price of a first-class stamp has remained relatively flat, not declined like virtually all goods and services on the market. And service quality has deteriorated. The Postal Service delivers a lesser-quality product at the same price, compared to the information technology standard of higher and higher quality products at lower and lower inflation-adjusted, or even nominal, prices. (Today's desktop computers, for example, have more power than the computers that traveled on the Apollo moon landing.)

In a competitive market, companies that fail to learn do not survive. In a protected environment, like the Postal Services', slow-learning organizations face irrelevance, as nimble competitors in nearby niches innovate around, over, and through the government-protected monopoly. The emergence of the Information Age thus accentuates the shortcomings of any monopoly.

Since 1971, the Postal Service has lost two key markets: overnight mail and parcel post. According to the General Accounting Office, as some competition was allowed, the USPS's share of the parcel post market fell from 65 percent 25 years ago to 6 percent in 1990 and for overnight delivery from 100 percent to 12 percent.

The question naturally arises: Why has not the explosion of electronic communications already supplanted the USPS? The answer may lie in a phenomenon first identified by Professor Paul David of Stanford University. He observed that during the first 40 years after introduction of electric motors into factories, productivity growth was relatively listless. It was not until the factories themselves evolved, adapting to individual electric motor–driven machines, from the central steam engines that early electric motors had replaced, that productivity surged.

A parallel can be seen today. With shipments of paper up 51 percent from 1983 to 1994, the country clearly is not moving to a fully electronic office. As *Bionomics* author Michael Rothschild writes:

> No one can say when all the critical elements of the Information Age infrastructure will come together. But it appears that we may be on the cusp of . . . completing the new office paradigm just as the unit drive motor completed the new factory paradigm of the 1920's. As communication technologies link the previously isolated power of microprocessors,

59

> the cost of delivering the right information where it is needed
> will collapse, allowing completely new work flows and organ-
> izational infrastructures to emerge.[3]

Indeed, one early result of the Information Age has been information overload. Information has expanded more rapidly than our
ability to process it. According to *Fortune*, from 1987 to mid 1994,
"information receptacles," such as e-mail, cellular phones, pagers,
faxes, voice mail, and answering machines, exploded from 41 million
to 149 million, even as we added 27 million new phone lines to an
existing base of 143 million. Only recently have information filters
emerged, products that help us prioritize, sort, and respond to e-mail,
and the like.

Dissemination of information ultimately will see a shift to a pull-
through capacity, with maximum consumer choice, that is, rather
than push-through. In the meantime, John Seely Brown, head of
Xerox PARC, suggests:

> It may be that we feel we're drowning in information because
> the information we're getting doesn't easily fit into our cur-
> rent mental models for understanding the world. The knowl-
> edge economy is fundamentally different from the industrial
> economy, and we haven't begun to come to terms with how
> different these two economies are.[4]

Not surprisingly, the market is responding. Document management software as well as text retrieval and workflow automation,
which currently total over $1 billion in sales per year, are projected
to grow at a 30 to 35 percent annual rate for the next few years.
Similar trends are seen in video and teleconferencing tools, e-mail,
and other devices to manage the flood of information that the microprocessor has made possible.

IBM's recent headline-grabbing purchase of Lotus Corporation
appears to have been motivated by a desire to acquire LotusNotes,
a program that creates a so-called rich text environment in which
documents, spreadsheets, and graphics are integrated. It is also plat-
form-independent; that is to say, it does not depend on whether
Notes clients are using PCs with Windows software or Macintosh
or other operating systems. To many, LotusNotes appears to be the
model, if not the emerging *de facto* standard, for a truly paperless
office.

Conclusion

In sum, while the distance between the paper-based "here" and the virtual "there" may seem great, the sheer magnitude of technological change and the relatively recent emergence of the Information Age itself suggest that the irrelevance of paper is a question of when, and not if. The challenge for policymakers is to recognize that the Information Age is here and that it differs fundamentally from the Machine Age. It is necessary to overcome what Massachusetts Institute of Technology's Mitchel Resnick calls "the centralized mindset." Complex results do not have to come about from central control, as is demonstrated by the Internet. From there, we can best establish the simple rules that will allow the Postal Service to evolve in its own right. Adapt and succeed, or fail to compete and fade away; either is preferable to the continued existence of a centralized, Machine Age Postal Service in a decentralized, Information Age world.

Notes

1. Daniel C. Roper, *The United States Post Office: Its Past Record, Present Condition, and Potential Relation to the New World Era* (New York: Funk & Wagnalls Co., 1917), p. 93.

2. Nicholas Negroponte, *Being Digital* (New York: Alfred A. Knoph, Inc., 1995), p. 181.

3. Michael Rothschild, "The Coming Productivity Surge." *Forbes ASAP*, March 1993, p. 18.

4. John Seely Brown, "Surviving Information Overload." *Fortune*, July 11, 1994, p. 65.

7. Natural Monopoly Myths: Lessons for Postal Service

Thomas J. DiLorenzo

> The very term "public utility".... is an absurd one. *Every* good is useful "to the public," and almost every good ... may be considered "necessary." Any designation of a few industries as "public utilities" is completely arbitrary and unjustified.
>
> —Murray Rothbard, *Power and Market*

The arguments for maintaining the monopoly status of the U.S. Postal Service are not unique to the mail delivery sector. More often these contentions are made concerning other so-called public utilities, for example, electricity, water, and gas. Supporters assert that those industries must be granted exclusive governmental franchise monopolies because they are "natural monopolies."

Put simply, a natural monopoly is said to occur when industries have relatively high fixed costs, such as expensive infrastructure or production technology. That means that their long-run average total costs decline as output expands. In such industries, the theory goes, a single producer eventually will be able to produce at a lower cost than any two other producers. Allowing more than one provider would increase costs for consumers. Competition could cause consumer inconvenience because of the construction of duplicative facilities, for example, several enterprises digging up the streets to put in dual gas or water lines. To avoid such costs and inconveniences, supporters contend that governments should grant single suppliers in such industries monopoly franchises. To head off price gouging by suppliers, the government must regulate prices. To make up for the lack of competition, the government must mandate which minimum services must be supplied to customers.

The author is professor of economics, Sellinger School of Business and Management, Loyola College in Baltimore, Maryland.

Today such arguments are used to support the U.S. Postal Service monopoly. But are they valid? In fact, for the very industries in which the arguments were most often applied in the past, markets are being liberalized and competition is lowering costs.

And were the arguments ever valid? It is a myth that natural monopoly theory was developed first by economists, and then used by legislators to justify franchise monopolies. Monopolies were created decades before the theory was formalized by intervention-minded policymakers, who then used the theory as an ex post facto rationale for government intervention. At the time the vast majority of economists understood that large-scale, capital-intensive production did not lead to monopoly, but was an absolutely desirable aspect of the competitive process.

The word "process" is important here. If competition is viewed as a dynamic, rivalrous process of entrepreneurship, then the fact that a single producer happens to have the lowest costs at any one time is of little consequence. The enduring forces of competition, including potential future competition, will render free-market monopoly an impossibility.

There is no historical basis for the theory of natural monopoly. Thus, those who use that theory in support of monopoly mail delivery stand on flawed and refuted premises.

Economies of Scale during the Franchise Monopoly Era

During the late 19th century, when local governments were beginning to grant franchise monopolies, the general economic understanding was that "monopoly" was caused by government intervention, not the free market, through franchises, protectionism, and other means. Large-scale production and economies of scale were seen as a competitive virtue, not a monopolistic vice. For example, Richard T. Ely, cofounder of the American Economic Association, wrote that "large-scale production is a thing which by no means necessarily signifies monopolized production."[1] John Bates Clark, Ely's cofounder, wrote in 1888 that the notion that industrial combinations would "destroy competition" should "not be too hastily accepted."[2]

Herbert Davenport of the University of Chicago advised in 1919 that only a few firms in an industry where there are economies of scale do not "require the elimination of competition,"[3] and his colleague, James Laughlin, noted that even when "a combination is large, a rival combination may give the most spirited competition."[4] Irving Fisher[5] and Edwin R. A. Seligman[6] both agreed that large-scale production produced *competitive* benefits through cost savings in advertising, selling, and less cross-shipping.

Large-scale production units unequivocally benefited the consumer, according to turn-of-the-century economists. For without large-scale production, according to Seligman, "the world would revert to a more primitive state of well being, and would virtually renounce the inestimable benefits of the best utilization of capital."[7] Simon Patten of the Wharton School expressed a similar view that "the combination of capital does not cause any economic disadvantage to the community. . . . Combinations are much more efficient than were the small producers whom they displaced."[8]

Like virtually every other economist of the day, Columbia's Franklin Giddings viewed competition much as the modern-day Austrian economists do, as a dynamic, rivalrous process. Consequently, he observed that "competition in some form is a permanent economic process. . . . Therefore, when market competition seems to have been suppressed, we should inquire what has become of the forces by which it was generated. We should inquire, further, to what degree market competition actually is suppressed or converted into other forms."[9] In other words, a "dominant" firm that underprices all its rivals at any point has not suppressed competition, for competition is "a permanent economic process."

David A. Wells, one of the most popular economic writers of the late 19th century, wrote that "the world demands abundance of commodities, and demands them cheaply; and experience shows that it can have them only by the employment of great capital upon extensive scale."[10] And George Gunton believed that "concentration of capital does not drive small capitalists out of business, but simply integrates them into larger and more complex systems of production, in which they are enabled to produce . . . more cheaply for the community and obtain a larger income for themselves. . . . Instead of concentration of capital tending to destroy competition the reverse is true. . . . By the use of large capital, improved machinery and better facilities the trust can and does undersell the corporation."[11]

The above quotations are not a selected, but rather a comprehensive, list. It may seem odd by today's standards, but as A. W. Coats pointed out, by the late 1880s there were only 10 men who had attained full-time professional status as economists in the United States.[12] Thus, the above quotations cover virtually every professional economist who had anything to say about the relationship between economies of scale and competitiveness at the turn of the century.

The significance of those views is that the men observed first hand the advent of large-scale production and did not see it leading to monopoly, "natural" or otherwise. In the spirit of the Austrian school, they understood that competition was an ongoing process, and that market dominance was always necessarily temporary in the absence of monopoly-creating government regulation.

That view is also consistent with my own research findings that the "trusts" of the late 19th century were in fact dropping their prices and expanding output faster than the rest of the economy—they were the most dynamic and competitive of all industries, not monopolists.[13] Perhaps that is why they were targeted by protectionist legislators and subjected to "antitrust" laws.

The economics profession came to embrace the theory of natural monopoly after the 1920s, when it became infatuated with "scientism" and adopted a more or less engineering theory of competition that categorized industries in terms of constant, decreasing, and increasing returns to scale (declining average total costs). According to this way of thinking, engineering relationships determined market structure and, consequently, competitiveness. The meaning of competition was no longer viewed as a behavioral phenomenon, but an engineering relationship. With the exception of such economists as Joseph Schumpeter, Ludwig von Mises, Friedrich Hayek, and other members of the Austrian School, the ongoing *process* of competitive rivalry and entrepreneurship was largely ignored.

How "Natural" Were the Early Natural Monopolies?

There is no evidence at all that at the outset of public utility regulation there existed any such phenomenon as a "natural monopoly." As Harold Demsetz has pointed out:

> Six electric light companies were organized in the one year of 1887 in New York City. Forty-five electric light enterprises had the legal right to operate in Chicago in 1907. Prior to 1895, Duluth, Minnesota, was served by five electric lighting

companies, and Scranton, Pennsylvania, had four in 1906. . . .
During the latter part of the nineteenth century, competition
was the usual situation in the gas industry in this country.
Before 1884, six competing companies were operating in New
York City. . . . Competition was common and especially per-
sistent in the telephone industry. . . . Baltimore, Chicago,
Cleveland, Columbus, Detroit, Kansas City, Minneapolis,
Philadelphia, Pittsburgh, and St. Louis, among the larger
cities, had at least two telephone services in 1905.[14]

In an extreme understatement, Demsetz concludes that "one
begins to doubt that scale economies characterized the utility industry at the time when regulation replaced market competition."[15]

A most instructive example of the nonexistence of natural monopoly in the utility industries is provided in a 1936 book by economist
George T. Brown entitled *The Gas Light Company of Baltimore,* which
bears the misleading subtitle, "A Study of Natural Monopoly."[16] The
book presents "the study of the evolutionary character of utilities"
in general, with special emphasis on the Gas Light Company of
Baltimore, the problems of which "are not peculiar either to the
Baltimore company or the State of Maryland, but are typical of those
met everywhere in the public utility industry."[17]

The history of the Gas Light Company of Baltimore figures promi-
nently in the whole history of natural monopoly, in theory and in
practice. The influential Richard T. Ely, who was a professor of
economics at Johns Hopkins University in Baltimore, chronicled the
company's problems in a series of articles in the *Baltimore Sun* that
were later published as a widely sold book.

The history of the Gas Light Company of Baltimore is that, from
its founding in 1816, it constantly struggled with new competitors.
Its response was not only to try to compete in the marketplace but
also to lobby the state and local government authorities to refrain
from granting corporate charters to its competitors. The company
operated with economics of scale, but that did not prevent numerous
competitors from cropping up.

"Competition is the life of business," the *Baltimore Sun* editorial-
ized in 1851 as it welcomed news of new competitors in the gas
light business.[18] The Gas Light Company of Baltimore, however,
"objected to the granting of franchise rights to the new company."[19]

But Brown misunderstood the implications of the case. He stated that "gas companies in other cities were exposed to ruinous competition," and then catalogued how those same companies sought desperately to enter the Baltimore market. But if such competition was so "ruinous," why would these companies enter new—and presumably just as "ruinous"—markets? Either Brown's theory of "ruinous competition"—which soon came to be the generally accepted one—was incorrect, or those companies were irrational gluttons for financial punishment.

By ignoring the *dynamic* nature of the competitive process, Brown made the same mistake that many other economists still make: believing that "excessive competition" can be "destructive" if low-cost producers drive their less efficient rivals from the market.[20] Such competition may be "destructive" to high-cost competitors, but it is beneficial to consumers.

In 1880 three competing gas companies in Baltimore competed fiercely with one another. They tried to merge and operate as a monopolist in 1888, but a new competitor foiled their plans: "Thomas Alva Edison introduced the electric light which threatened the existence of all gas companies."[21] From that point on there was competition between both gas and electric companies, all of which incurred heavy fixed costs that led to economies of scale. Nevertheless, no free-market or "natural" monopoly ever materialized.

When monopoly did appear, it was solely because of government intervention. For example, in 1890 a bill was introduced into the Maryland legislature that "called for an annual payment to the city from the Consolidated [Gas Company] of $10,000 a year and 3% of all dividends declared in return for the privilege of enjoying a twenty-five year monopoly."[22] This is the now-familiar approach of government officials colluding with industry executives to establish a monopoly that will gouge the consumers, and then sharing the loot with the politicians in the form of franchise fees and taxes on monopoly revenues. This approach is especially pervasive today in the cable television industry.

Legislative "regulation" of gas and electric companies produced the predictable result of monopoly prices, about which the public complained bitterly. Rather than deregulating the industry and letting competition control prices, however, public utility regulation was adopted supposedly to appease the consumers who, according to Brown, "felt that the negligent manner in which their interests were being served [by legislative control of gas and electric prices] resulted in high rates and monopoly privileges. *The development of utility regulation in Maryland typified the experience of other states*"[23] (emphasis added). Here the parallel with the Postal Service is obvious. The Postal Service must secure approval of the U.S. Postal Rate Commission to raise prices.

Not all economists were fooled by the "natural monopoly" theory advocated by utility industry monopolists and their paid economic advisers. In 1940 economist Horace M. Gray, an assistant dean of the graduate school at the University of Illinois, surveyed the history of "the public utility concept." He concluded that with state grants of special privilege, "The final result was monopoly, exploitation, and political corruption."[24] With regard to "public" utilities, Gray records that "between 1907 and 1938, the policy of state-created, state-protected monopoly became firmly established over a significant portion of the economy and became the keystone of modern public utility regulation."[25] From that time on, "the public utility status was to be the haven of refuge for all aspiring monopolists who found it too difficult, too costly, or too precarious to secure and maintain monopoly by private action alone."[26]

The would-be monopolists included the radio, real estate, milk, air transport, coal, oil, and agricultural industries. And they had the Post Office as a model.

Many economists constructed what Gray called a "confused rationalization" for "the sinister forces of private privilege and monopoly" to justify government-granted monopolies.[27]

More recent economic research supports Gray's analysis. In one of the first statistical studies of the effects of rate regulation in the electric utilities industry, published in 1962, George Stigler and Claire Friedland found no significant differences in prices and profits of utilities with and without regulatory commissions from 1917 to 1932.[28] Early rate regulators *did not* help the consumer, but rather were "captured" by the industry, as happened in so many other industries, from trucking to airlines to cable television.

Sixteen years after the Stigler-Friedland study, Gregg Jarrell observed that when, between 1912 and 1917, some 25 state governments substituted their own electric power rates for municipal regulation, rates rose by 46 percent and profits by 38 percent, while output levels fell by 23 percent.[29] Thus, municipal regulation failed to hold prices down. Utilities successfully lobbied for state regulation under the theory that state regulators would be less pressured by local customer groups than mayors and city councils would be.

The Problem of "Excessive Duplication"

Another reason given by proponents for granting monopoly franchises is that too many competitors disrupt communities, for example, by allowing several different water suppliers, electric power producers, or cable TV operators to dig up the streets, or perhaps by causing fleets of delivery trucks from competing private mail services to descend on those streets. But as Harold Demsetz has observed:

> The problem of excessive duplication of distributions systems is attributable to the failure of communities to set a proper price on the use of these scarce resources. The right to use publicly owned thoroughfares is the right to use a scarce resource. The absence of a price for the use of these resources, a price high enough to reflect the opportunity costs of such alternative uses as the servicing of uninterrupted traffic and unmarred views, will lead to their overutilization. The setting of an appropriate fee for the use of these resources would reduce the degree of duplication to optimal levels.[30]

The "duplication" problem is caused by governments that own the streets under which utility lines are placed, and fail to price these resources appropriately. Under private ownership of streets and sidewalks, which is more and more the case in condominium housing developments today, owners can trade off lower utility prices for the temporary inconvenience of having a utility company run a trench through their property.

The Natural Monopoly Myth: Electric Utilities

According to natural monopoly theory, competition cannot persist in the electric utility industry. As this is one of the toughest cases, if it can be refuted, it can be implied that there is even less of a case for a monopoly for mail delivery. Electric utility competition has in fact persisted for decades in dozens of U.S. cities. In his 1986 book, *Direct Utility Competition: The Natural Monopoly Myth*, economist

Walter J. Primeaux Jr. concludes the following concerning cities where there is direct competition in the electric utility industries:

- Direct rivalry between two competing firms has existed for very long periods of time—for over 80 years in some cities;
- The rival electric utilities compete vigorously through prices and services;
- Customers have gained substantial benefits from the competition, compared with cities where there are electric utility monopolies;
- Contrary to natural monopoly theory, costs are actually lower where two firms operate;
- Contrary to natural monopoly theory, there is no more excess capacity under competition than under monopoly in the electric utility industry;
- Any consumer satisfaction problems caused by dual power lines are considered by consumers to be less significant than the benefits from competition.[31]

Primeaux also found that although electric utility executives generally recognized the consumer benefits of competition, they personally preferred monopoly!

Ten years after the publication of Primeaux's book, at least one state—California—is transforming its electric utility industry "from a monopoly controlled by a handful of publicly held utilities to an open market."[32] Other states are moving in the same direction, finally abandoning the baseless theory of natural monopoly in favor of natural competition:[33]

- The Ormet Corporation, an aluminum smelter in West Virginia, obtained state permission to solicit competitive bids from 40 electric utilities;
- Alcan Aluminum Corporation in Oswego, New York, has taken advantage of technological breakthroughs that allowed it to build a new power-generating plant next to its mill, cutting its power costs by two-thirds. Niagara Mohawk, its previous and higher-priced power supplier, is suing the state to prohibit Alcan from using its own power;
- Arizona political authorities allowed Cargill, Inc., to buy power from anywhere in the West; the company expects to save $8 million per year;
- New federal laws permit utilities to import lower-priced power, using the power lines of other companies to transport it;

- Wisconsin Public Service commissioner Scott Neitzel recently declared, "Free markets are the best mechanism for delivering to the consumer . . . the best service at the lowest cost;"
- The prospect of future competition is already forcing some electric utility monopolies to cut their costs and prices.
- When the Tennessee Valley Authority was faced with competition from Duke Power in 1988, it managed to hold its rates steady without an increase for the next several years.

The potential benefits to the U.S. economy from demonopolization of the electric utility industry are enormous. Competition will initially save consumers at least $40 billion per year, according to utility economist Robert Michaels.[34]

Of course, the technology and infrastructure necessary to transmit electricity is more complex and disruptive than that needed to transfer pieces of paper from one location to another. One thus would suspect that inasmuch as the problems of establishing a free market for electricity with competing suppliers can be overcome, a market for mail delivery would be even easier to establish.

The Natural Monopoly Myth: Cable TV

Cable television is also a franchise monopoly in most cities. But the monopolies in this industry are anything but "natural." They are mandated by governments. Yet as with electricity, there are dozens of cities in the United States where there are competing cable firms. As University of California, Davis economist and former Federal Communications Commission chief economist Thomas Hazlett observes, "Direct competition. . .currently occurs in at least three dozen jurisdictions nationally."[35] Although cable operators complain of "duplication," it is important to keep in mind that "while overbuilding an existing cable system can lower the profitability of the incumbent operator, it unambiguously improves the position of consumers who face prices determined not by historical costs, but by the interplay of supply and demand."[36]

Where there are competing cable companies prices are about 23 percent below those of monopolistic cable operators.[37] Cablevision of Central Florida, for example, reduced its basic prices from $12.95 to $6.50 per month in "duopoly" areas to compete. When Telestat entered Riviera Beach, Florida, it offered 26 channels of basic service for $5.75, compared with Comcast's 12-channel offering for $8.40 per month. Comcast responded by upgrading its service and dropping its prices.[38] In Presque Isle, Maine, when the city government invited competition, the incumbent firm quickly upgraded its service from only 12 channels to 54 channels.[39]

In 1987 the Pacific West Cable Company sued the city of Sacramento, California, on First Amendment grounds for blocking its entry into the cable market. A jury found that "the Sacramento cable market was not a natural monopoly and that the claim of natural monopoly was a sham used by defendants as a pretext for granting a single cable television franchise . . . to promote the making of cash payments and provision of 'in-kind' services . . . and to obtain increased campaign contributions."[40] The city was forced to adopt a competitive cable policy, the result of which was for the incumbent cable operator, Scripps Howard, to drop its monthly price from $14.50 to $10.00 to meet a competitor's price. The company also offered free installation and three months' free service in every area where it had competition.

Still, most cable systems in the United States are franchise monopolies that benefit cable companies, who share the loot with the politicians through campaign contributions, free air time on "community service programming," contributions to local foundations favored by the politicians, stock equity and consulting contracts to the politically well connected, and various gifts to the franchise authorities.

It is instructive to note that, based on the premise that the broadcast spectrum is a limited resource, the federal government has owned it as a monopoly and licensed it out for use by particular stations. But even before the advent of cable the nearly 90 UHF stations in any region of the country were devoid of programming. Cable, of course, expanded capacity even further, offering competition to spectrum broadcasters. And satellite dishes add another competitor to the market.

Just as technological advances discredited the excuse for a spectrum monopoly, e-mail, faxes, and the Internet do so for the argument that there are no alternatives to a government monopoly on mail delivery.

Conclusions

The theory of natural monopoly is an economic fiction. No such thing as a "natural" monopoly has ever existed. In the late 19th and early 20th centuries public utilities competed vigorously, to the benefit of consumers. But various service providers wanting protection from competition secured government-sanctioned monopolies. Only later did economists construct an ex post facto rationalization for their monopoly power.

But today, in industry after industry, the natural monopoly concept is finally eroding. Electric power, cable TV, telephone services, and the mails are all on the verge of being deregulated, either legislatively or de facto, because of technological change. The failures of the U.S. Postal Service are apparent. But its supporters still cling to old natural monopoly theory, even as competition from e-mail, faxes, the Internet, and private delivery services show this theory to be ludicrous. The natural monopoly fiction of the 19th century, establishing monopolistic privileges, has no place in the 21st century. Neither does a government postal service.

Notes

1. Richard T. Ely, *Monopolies and Trusts* (New York: Macmillan, 1900), p. 162.

2. John Bates Clark and Franklin Giddings, *Modern Distributive Processes* (Boston: Ginn & Co., 1888), p. 21.

3. Herbert Davenport, *The Economics of Enterprise* (New York: Macmillan, 1919), p. 483.

4. James L. Laughlin, *The Elements of Political Economy* (New York: American Book Co., 1902), p. 71.

5. Irving Fisher, *Elementary Principles of Economics* (New York: Macmillan, 1912), p. 330.

6. E. R. A. Seligman, *Principles of Economics* (New York: Longmans, Green & Co., 1909), p. 341.

7. Ibid., p. 97.

8. Simon Patten, "The Economic Effects of Combinations," *Age of Steel*, Jan. 5, 1889, p. 13.

9. Franklin Giddings, "The Persistence of Competition," *Political Science Quarterly*, March 1887, p. 62.

10. David A. Wells, *Recent Economic Changes* (New York: DeCapro Press, 1889), p. 74.

11. George Gunton, "The Economics and Social Aspects of Trusts," *Political Science Quarterly*, September 1888, p. 385.

12. A. W. Coats, "The American Political Economy Club," *American Economic Review*, September 1961, pp. 621–37.

13. Thomas J. DiLorenzo, "The Origins of Antitrust: An Interest-Group Perspective," *International Review of Law and Economics* (Fall 1985): 73–90.

14. Burton N. Behling, *Competition and Monopoly in Public Utility Industries* (1938), cited in Harold Demsetz, *Efficiency, Competition, and Policy* (Cambridge, Mass.: Blackwell, 1989), p. 78.

15. Ibid.

16. George T. Brown, *The Gas Light Company of Baltimore: A Study of Natural Monopoly* (Baltimore: Johns Hopkins University Press, 1936).

17. Ibid., p. 5.

18. Ibid., p. 31.

19. Ibid.

20. Ibid., p. 47.

21. Ibid., p. 52.

22. Ibid., p. 75.

23. Ibid., p. 106.

24. Ibid.

25. Ibid., p. 9.

26. Ibid.

27. Ibid., p. 11.

28. George Stigler and Claire Friedland, "What Can Regulators Regulate? The Case of Electricity," *Journal of Law and Economics*, Oct. 1962, 1–16.

29. Gregg A. Jarrell, "The Demand for State Regulation of the Electric Utility Industry," *Journal of Law and Economics*, Oct. 1978, 269–95.

30. Demsetz, p. 81.

31. Walter J. Primeaux Jr., *Direct Electric Utility Competition: The Natural Monopoly Myth* (New York: Praeger, 1986), p. 175.

32. "California Eyes Open Electricity Market," *Washington Times*, May 27, 1995, p. 2.

33. The following information is from Toni Mack, "Power to the People," *Forbes*, June 5, 1995, pp. 119–26.

34. Ibid., p. 120.

35. Thomas Hazlett, "Duopolistic Competition in Cable Television: Implications for Public Policy," *Yale Journal on Regulation* 7 (1990): 35.

36. Ibid., p. 69.

37. Ibid., p. 90.

38. Ibid., pp. 93–94.

39. Thomas Hazlett, "Private Contracting versus Public Regulation as a Solution to the Natural Monopoly Problem," in *Unnatural Monopolies: The Case for Deregulating Public Utilities*, ed. Robert W. Poole (Lexington, Mass.: Lexington Books, 1985), p. 104.

40. *Pacific West Cable Co. vs. City of Sacramento*, 672 F. Supp. 1322, 1349–50 (E.D. Cal. 1987), cited in Hazlett, "Duopolistic Competition," p. 103.

PART III

MARKET STRUCTURES FOR PRIVATE DELIVERY

8. Patterns of Private Delivery

R. Richard Geddes

> Thus, within 50 years of the birth of the nation, the postal
> industry was well established, but competition threatened
> the postal monopoly because of high postal rates and defi-
> ciencies in service. Legislation was required to maintain the
> monopoly. The postal service was not a natural monopoly
> in 1845 in the sense that it would not serve as a predominant
> supplier if subject to the competitive marketplace; the
> monopoly was forced through legislation. The 1970 Postal
> Reorganization Act continued the enforced monopoly. . . .
> Today again, as in the 1840s, there is a challenge to the postal
> monopoly. This time caused in part by new technologies.
>
> U.S. Department of Commerce, 1977[1]

Today, one can write a letter on a personal computer, upload it
into electronic mail and send it instantaneously anywhere in the
world. Or one can print out or hand-write that same letter and fax
it, again instantaneously. Or one can contract with United Parcel
Service or Federal Express to deliver the letter overnight. However,
one cannot legally contract with a private delivery service, at lower
cost, to deliver that same letter at slower speeds. The Private Express
Statutes forbid any such private contracting.[2]

Almost 20 years ago researchers at the Department of Commerce
recognized that the monopoly, forced by law, was threatened by
competition, and had little to do with "natural monopoly." They
also recognized that evolving technologies provided a strong reason
to reexamine the monopoly. Because the technology has now largely
evolved, it seems appropriate again to review carefully the rationale
for and effects of the monopoly the United States Postal Service
(USPS) has over the carriage of letter mail. Such a review is facilitated

The author is an assistant professor in economics at Fordham University. He wishes
to thank the Earhard Foundation for support of research presented in this chapter.

by a consideration of the implications of repeal of the USPS's monopoly status, and how, in this case, the private delivery market might be structured.

The Structure of Mail Flows

To appreciate the meaning of demonopolization of postal services, it is valuable to consider the composition of current mail flows, and particularly the extent of personal letter delivery within them. Of particular interest to many consumers is the use of the mails simply to send a letter or card to a friend or relative, that is, household-to-household mail. When most consumers think of a delivery market, they have this in mind.

The proportion of total USPS mail flows composed of this mail is shrinking. For example, in 1991 all household-to-household mail made up only 8.4 percent of total mail flows.[3] Some 3.3 percent of all mail was correspondence, while 4.9 percent was greeting cards.[4] In 1977, total household-to-household mail comprised 12 percent of total mail flows, implying relative shrinkage of this category. Thus, the vast majority of total mail flows is composed of communications sent from businesses to households, such as advertising matter, making up 44.3 percent in 1991; mail sent from households to businesses, such as payment of bills, making up 15.4 percent in 1991; and mail sent from businesses to other businesses, 31.5 percent in 1991.[5]

It is likely that, in 1996, the proportion of mail composed of personal correspondence is even smaller. Thus, the market that is of most concern to the majority of consumers is actually a small and decreasing part of total Postal Service volume. An extremely large organization is maintained as a monopoly in its core businesses to support mainly bill payment and the delivery of advertising matter, as well as governmental material. When considering how a private market might operate, it is thus important to note first, that the institutional market is substantially larger than the household-to-household market, and second, that the household-to-household market may be structured differently from the institutional market.

Natural Monopoly Concerns

One argument against postal competition is that mail delivery is a "natural monopoly." This is the notion that one large firm is the most efficient, least-cost supplier of a good, that the firm must be rate-regulated to price efficiently and not gouge consumers, and that the firm must be given an exclusive geographic franchise to prevent "wasteful competition."[6] Yet natural monopoly arguments, both in economic theory and, more important, in actual deregulatory experience, have been discredited, especially as they relate to the postal market. There are at least four powerful reasons for this.

First, while there are undoubtedly scale economies in some aspects of postal services, such as the local distribution network, postal services do not have the extensive fixed-cost requirements of industries typically characterized as natural monopolies, such as electric and gas utilities, which require extensive pipe or wire facilities to distribute their products.[7]

Second, capital used in postal services is mobile. For example, trucks literally can be driven into new markets or contracted for, sorting centers can be accommodated easily in a variety of commercial properties, and semiskilled labor for sorting and delivery appears to be in surplus throughout the country. Thus, delivery businesses can move rapidly into new markets and eliminate any excess profits made by existing firms. Additionally, the high capital mobility increases the *threat* of competition from other firms, giving postal services characteristics of a contestable market.[8]

Third, the experience in delivery services suggests that a competitive private market will evolve. Where private firms such as Federal Express and United Parcel Service have been allowed to compete directly with the USPS, such as in overnight delivery and parcel post, those markets have turned out to be highly competitive.

Fourth, the actual deregulatory experience in other related industries suggests that postal services will not tend to natural monopoly, but rather that competition will be substantial. For example, the closely related "network" industry of trucking was deregulated in the late 1970s.[9] The industry is now very competitive, with a variety of choices for shippers, and the consensus among academic economists is that deregulation was a resounding success, with lower rates, lower costs and better service, and more choice.[10] The experience with airline deregulation is similarly successful. Moreover, industries facing higher fixed costs, such as long-distance telephones and gas pipelines, have been successfully deregulated, with concomitant benefits to consumers. Indeed, it appears that even electric utilities are likely to face competition at the retail residential level, perhaps as early as the end of the century.

Therefore, concerns that a private postal market would become monopolistic are unfounded. Indeed, it appears that postal services are more competitive than some industries that already have been successfully deregulated. This insight is used below in analyzing the vertical structure of postal services.

Vertical Integration versus Market Contracting

An important question regarding the expected pattern of private delivery services is the nature of the vertical structure of postal services. In postal services, the main functions include pickup, mail processing, such as inward sortation, facing, canceling, and outward sortation, and delivery. If a firm is vertically integrated, all these functions are owned by that firm. The USPS is currently a highly vertically integrated organization.[11] It owns almost all the capital required to perform those functions, contracting only with labor. Because of its monopolized nature, there is no a priori reason to believe that that is the most efficient organizational structure for postal delivery services.

The basic theoretical considerations of vertical integration lie in Nobel Prize–winning economist Ronald Coase's seminal work on the firm.[12] Simply put, if the costs of transacting are high, firms will conserve on these costs and will vertically integrate; that is, they will merge. Where transactions costs are low, the firms will rely on market contracting. The substance of the theory lies in identifying and measuring transactions costs. Numerous important aspects of transactions costs have been identified. Two aspects identified and developed in detail by Oliver Williamson are opportunistic behavior and asset specificity.[13]

Opportunistic Behavior

One type of transactions cost is referred to as "opportunism." Williamson states:

> By opportunism I mean self-interest seeking with guile. This includes but is scarcely limited to more blatant forms, such as lying, stealing, and cheating. Opportunism more often involves subtle forms of deceit. Both active and passive forms and both *ex ante* and *ex post* types are included.[14]

Opportunism is relevant because it increases the uncertainty associated with, and thus raises the cost of, contracting for services outside the firm rather than performing the service in house. Higher contracting costs will, all else being equal, decrease the amount of contracting and increase the probability of vertical integration. Dealings that have substantial potential opportunism are more likely to be vertically integrated.

Concerning postal services, one might expect that more rapid delivery would magnify the potential for opportunism, because more is at stake in delaying services to another firm in the process, say between a delivery and a sorting firm. Greater time pressure for delivery increases the threat that one or both parties will exploit the other, and thus increase contracting costs.

Asset Specificity

Asset specificity refers to the notion that assets at times must be tailored to a particular transaction. That is, there are idiosyncratic aspects of transactions that have implications for transactions costs. In a well-known example, General Motors (GM) contracted with Fisher Body to make car bodies specifically for GM cars. This implied that manufacturing equipment owned by Fisher Body had to be tailored to its contract with GM.

If assets must be tailored to a particular transaction, then one or both parties has some amount of investment sunk into the transaction, which increases the chance that ex post facto, one party may try to exploit the other. That increases the uncertainty associated with transactions costs and therefore increases the likelihood that vertical integration will take place.

For postal services, the degree of asset specificity is likely to increase as speed and reliability of delivery increase. That is because the assets of contracting parties must be more closely tailored to each other to ensure rapid turnover of mail.

Describing Postal Pricing

Two of the principal attributes of postal delivery services that are of interest to the consumer are reliability and speed of delivery. Customers appear to value reliability highly and demand a high level of guaranteed delivery across a large range of services. This is intuitively sensible: if consumers invest the time and energy to prepare materials and address and package them, they want them to reach their destination with a high probability. Evidence of the

Figure 1

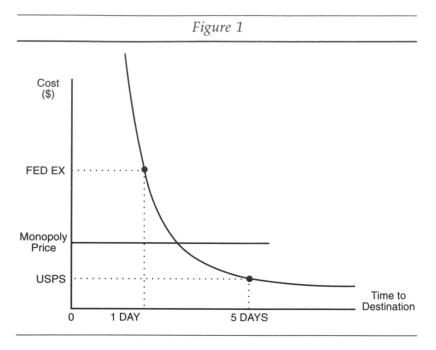

reliability preference can be seen in the recent cases of the USPS snooping on private enterprises to determine whether they were sending only "extremely urgent" material in Federal Express packages. The Postal Service maintained that many of the packages did not contain time-sensitive material. If that is so, customers could only have been paying higher overnight rates to obtain the higher level of reliability associated with private services.

Given a high, constant level of reliability, costs of delivery will vary directly with the desired speed of delivery, or inversely with the time to destination, and can be described graphically.

In Figure 1, the time to destination, or the "slowness" of delivery, appears on the horizontal axis, while costs of achieving that speed appear on the vertical. In this figure, the costs of delivery approach infinity as the time of delivery approaches zero. That is, if physical delivery of a letter across the country in one minute is desired, all available resources could not achieve that end. Conversely, if the time to delivery approaches infinity, that is, if the letter is never delivered, the cost approaches zero. Figure 1 simply assumes that there is a range of speeds between infinitely fast and not delivering at all, which suggests the shape shown here. If a higher level of reliability is desired, the entire curve will shift upward, and, as noted, it appears that a high uniform level of reliability is desired by most users.

Given free entry into postal services, as noted above, a highly competitive market is likely to evolve. The implication is that there will be entry at different cost levels along the curve in Figure 1. Currently, entry is legally allowed only at the high end of the speed/cost curve; that is, next-day air services and the like are exempt from the Private Express Statutes. The USPS's monopoly is enforced over the low-speed end of the curve, thus preventing low-cost and, under competitive conditions, low-priced service firms from entering the market.

The Results of Competition

If the Private Express Statutes establishing the mail monopoly were repealed, several results are likely. One is this:

The postal market likely would be stratified by speed of delivery, with competition in each stratum, and a high level of overall reliability.

Simply put, numerous overnight services will still exist, but also many lower-cost, slower, but still reliable services. They might include inexpensive three-, four-, and five-day guaranteed delivery services.

Further implications can be drawn by considering this insight in light of the understanding that firms are more likely to be vertically integrated if there are chances for opportunistic behavior and asset specificity. As noted, faster delivery is likely to increase contracting problems associated with both opportunism and specific assets. If delivery is guaranteed within a very short time, assets must be tailored to the needs of the delivery company. For example, an airline might be required to adjust its flight schedule to the needs of the high-speed company using its services. Additionally, to ensure rapid movement of material, it may be necessary to tailor aircraft so that they are compatible with the trucks of the high-speed firm, which further increases asset specificity. In this instance, contracting costs are likely to be quite high. However, if speed is not such a crucial consideration, then delivery assets need not be nearly so tailored to the specifics of the pick-up, processing, or delivery firms,

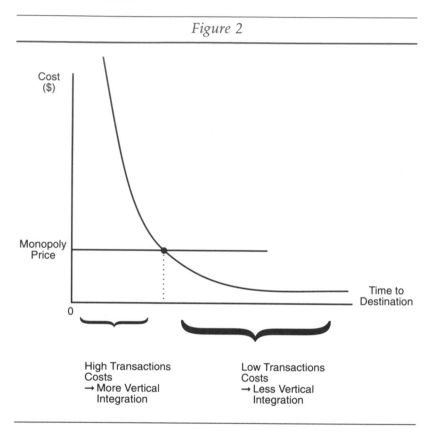

Figure 2

and contracting costs are likely to be lower. Therefore, there would be *more* vertical integration of firms at the higher-speed, higher-cost levels of delivery than at the slower speeds.[15] Such a situation is illustrated in Figure 2:

Figure 2 shows that higher contracting costs, and thus more vertical integration, are associated with higher speed services, which gives rise to another result:

High-speed delivery services are more likely to be vertically integrated, while low-speed services are more likely to rely on contracting between firms.

This result of competition has important implications for the expected efficiency of the current fully vertically integrated organization of the USPS, which dominates the low-speed, low-cost end of the curve.[16] The analysis suggests that the efficiency losses associated with that organizational arrangement are extremely high, and that substantial savings could be obtained by having separately owned firms contracting with one another to provide low-speed service. The savings through improved organizational efficiency would be captured through a lower overall price of delivery.

Other Implications
Note on Transactions Costs and Pricing

Some commentators have suggested that private delivery systems would be inefficient because they would price according to customer density, and that would result in excessively confusing pricing systems. However, competitive providers have an incentive to take that cost into account, and will be rewarded for simple pricing schemes. United Parcel Service, for example, prices its package services according to "zone," or distance from the origin, and thus ignores density of destination altogether. Within certain broad limits, overnight services are similar. Prices are the same for broadly defined zones and ignore density. Firms providing less time-sensitive delivery would probably price in a similar manner.

Note on Equity

The argument also has been made that the deregulation of delivery services would hurt the poor, since they are unable to afford either a fax machine or expensive overnight services. But it must be kept in mind that the exception to the Private Express Statutes mandates that overnight services not bring their prices down so low that they compete with first-class letter mail. The exception thus *mandates* that prices for private delivery remain high. This turns the argument that "the poor cannot afford private postal services, and they must remain socialized" on its head. The law specifically requires that prices remain high. The analysis presented here suggests that, because of a range of costs over delivery speed, a diversity of services is likely to be offered under competition. Thus, customers on a tight budget will be offered a range of services in a deregulated market that meets their budgetary constraints.[17] As in other industries, such as trucking, deregulation helps the poor by lowering prices.

Conclusion

The analysis presented here shows that deregulation of postal services will result in a highly competitive market, stratified by speed of delivery, with a high uniform level of reliability. Because of the presence of specific assets and the potential for opportunism, high-speed services are more likely to be vertically integrated, while private low-speed delivery services, currently outlawed, are more likely to use contracting between pickup, processing, and delivery functions. The USPS now monopolizes the low-speed end of the speed/cost relation, but allows competition in the high-speed. However, the USPS is an almost completely vertically integrated firm. This analysis therefore implies that there are substantial gains to be obtained from disintegration, or divestiture, of various divisions, and that this would be likely to occur in a competitive market.

Notes

1. Donald R. Ewing and Roger K. Salaman, "The Postal Crisis: The Postal Function as a Communications Service," Department of Commerce, Office of Telecommunications, Special publication 77-13, 1977.

2. See U.S. Postal Service, "Statutes Restricting Private Carriage of Mails and Their Administration," House Committee on Post Office and Civil Service, 93rd Cong., 1st sess., Committee Print. Throughout this paper, "the monopoly" will refer to the ability of the Postal Service to exclude competitors from carrying first- and third-class mail as defined in the aforementioned document.

3. See George S. Tolley, "Direct Testimony of George S. Tolley on Behalf of United States Postal Service," USPS-T-2, Docket No. R94-1, 1994, p. 28.

4. Both numbers are rounded off.

5. Previously mentioned. To avoid cumbersome language, the term "business" is used here to mean all nonhousehold material, and thus includes nonprofit and governmental mail.

6. See W. Kip Viscusi, J. M. Vernon, and J. E. Harrington, Economics of Regulation and Antitrust (Lexington: D.C. Heath and Company, 1992).

7. See Cathy M. Rogerson and William M. Takis, "Economies of Scale and Scope and Competition in Postal Services," in Regulation and the Nature of Postal Services, ed. Michael A. Crew and Paul R. Kleindorfer, (Boston: Kluwer Academic Publishers, 1992). Note that natural monopoly was not a justification for the original monopoly. In fact, the Private Express Statutes were enacted to suppress competition from private firms, such as Wells-Fargo and the Pony Express.

8. See W. J. Baumol, J. C. Panzer, and R. D. Willig, Contestable Markets and the Theory of Industry Structure (San Diego: Harcourt Brace Jovanavich, 1982).

9. I believe that the relation between trucking and postal services is underappreciated. Both require trucks, sorting centers, and similar types of labor, and are network industries. The deregulatory experience of trucking is thus highly relevant for postal services.

10. For a summary of this literature, see W. Kip Viscusi, J. M. Vernon, and J. E. Harrington, Economics of Regulation and Antitrust (Lexington: D.C. Heath and Company, 1992), chapter 17.

11. There are important exceptions, such as contracting for delivery on rural carrier routes.

12. See Ronald H. Coase, "The Nature of the Firm," *Economica* N.S.4 (1937).

13. See, for example, Oliver E. Williamson, *The Economic Institutions of Capitalism* (New York: Free Press, 1985), or Oliver E. Williamson, *Markets and Hierarchies: Analysis and Implications for Antitrust* (1975).

14. See Williamson, (*The Economic Institutions of Capitalism*), p. 47.

15. This is not to deny that substantial amounts of contracting will not, and in fact do not now, occur at the relatively high-speed delivery levels. It merely serves to further buttress my conclusion that there will be substantial amounts of vertical disintegration, and large amounts of contracting, at slower delivery speeds.

16. Union pressure often ensures that this is the case. Witness the high level of resistance by the union to any form of contracting out for services, which is simply the USPS attempting to vertically disintegrate.

17. The experience with deregulation in other industries, such as trucking and airlines, supports this conclusion, as does common sense. The view that "you can have any color car you want, as long as it is black" rarely long persists under competitive conditions.

9. Competition in Postal Service: International Perspectives

Michael A. Crew

Competition, innovation, technological change, and deregulation have profoundly affected most industries in most countries throughout the world. In some cases, technology has been the driving force, most notably in telecommunications, with the microelectronics revolution and accompanying rapid changes in hardware and attendant software. In others cases, the forces of competition and innovation have had the major impact—for example, the role of Federal Express in revolutionizing courier service.

Government-owned, -operated, or -protected postal services worldwide have not remained islands in a sea of chance, insulated from these pressures. Yet until recently they have not found it necessary to make major course corrections or transform themselves as a result of competition. This situation is now changing. A review of postal services in other countries shows that economic pressures are pushing them toward more market-based approaches.

Postal Service and Other Infrastructure

A traditional reason used to justify government's granting monopoly status to a particular service provider is that the service is a natural monopoly. That is to say, the assumption is that smaller competitors cannot provide the service as efficiently as can one large supplier. A further argument is that without government regulation, a large single supplier would gouge consumers. But that argument never was as strong for mail delivery as it was for other network industries such as telecommunications, gas, water, and electricity. At first sight, postal service is more like trucking and airlines, with very little capital sunk in a network. Postal service is the most labor

The author is a professor and the chair of the Finance-Economics Department, and director of the Center for Research in Regulated Industries at Rutgers University.

intensive of all those industries. In the case of the U.S. Postal Service, about 80 percent of its costs are represented by labor.

Airline deregulation offers lessons for the future of postal service. With deregulation the market has experienced major changes. Major players have departed the scene over the past 15 years, notably People's Express, Pan American, and Eastern Airlines. And that has occurred in an industry in which rapid technological change has not had an obvious effect. At least for a major input of the industry, aircraft, there have not been major technological advances. The larger manufacturers, Boeing, McDonnel-Douglas, and Airbus, have made some important design changes. But there has been no quantum leap equivalent to the jet engine's introduction on passenger aircraft over the past four decades, or the microelectronic and fiber optic developments in telecommunications. There may have been improvements in fuel economy but attributes such as speed, the quality of cabin air, and seat comfort have remained unchanged or even deteriorated. The Supersonic Transport or SST, developed in the 1960s and early 1970s, has been a commercial flop, operating out of only a few airports.

In the United States, major deregulation of airlines and routes, beginning in the late 1970s, meant more flights. But inefficient government-owned and -operated air traffic control has been stretched to capacity to meet new demand. Further, government-owned airports, bound by antiquated federal regulations, have had a difficult time handling the increased volume. The main technological change has been in pricing innovations brought about by advanced reservation systems that combine telecommunications and computers.

Labor Costs

Despite the relatively slow technological innovations, there have been major changes in the way the airline industry does business. Labor costs have been put under pressure. Wages have been reduced and some labor practices changed in an attempt to raise productivity. Postal service is, in this sense, similar to airlines, with labor costs high as a proportion of expenditures. Economists Michael L. Wachter and Jeffrey M. Perloff estimate that the U.S. Postal Service pays a significant premium over the market wage. For purposes of comparing postal wages with the rest of the economy, their study examines the effect of unions not only on the postal sector but elsewhere in the U.S. and UK economies. They state:

> Our results support the existence of a postal premium in the United States of approximately 21 per cent. . . . The British Post Office pays a slight wage premium compared to the private sector . . . of approximately 6 per cent.[1]

The lesson from the airlines for postal services throughout the world is that competition will affect their costs, especially for labor, and their ways of doing business. When faced with competition, postal services throughout the world will attack labor costs, cutting payrolls by attrition, layoffs, and accelerated retirements, in addition to reducing benefits and perhaps wage rates. The unions are fully aware of these developments and are likely to be a major if not the major force opposing change.[2]

Stranded Costs

While the experiences of airlines provide postal services a view of likely effects of competition on labor costs, telecommunications, electricity, and gas deregulation also provide important lessons. Indeed, despite high labor intensity, postal services do share some important features with traditional utilities. Unlike airlines and trucking but in common with telephone, gas, and electricity they have scale economies in local distribution, giving the arguments for government's granting and regulating monopolies some seeming validity. Local postal delivery networks display scale economies. Competitors wish to have access to them just as competitive long-distance telephone carriers and independent generators seek access, respectively, to the local telephone company's network and the electric utilities' transmission and distribution system. Just as the pricing of access is a major issue in a more competitive utility sector, so it is in the postal sector. For postal services, access pricing concerns the types of discounts and service options that private companies are given by postal monopolies.

Exactly how to set prices for access to the systems is the subject of a major debate in the United States in electricity, telecommunications, and gas. In the electric utility industry, that is a particularly difficult issue because of the existence of the problem of so-called stranded costs or assets. Put in simple terms, this means that part of the investment made by the utility is underutilized. Electric utilities invest both in plant facilities to generate power and in cables, wires, and other infrastructure necessary to transmit the power. They calculate income and profit on the basis of the mix of investments. If private competitors generate power and sell it to users over the public utility's wires, the utility forgoes income from generating power.

One proposal for recovering the stranded costs involves a form of access pricing called efficient component pricing. William J. Baumol and J. Gregory Sidak would define this approach as equating input prices with average-incremental cost, including all pertinent incremental opportunity costs.[3] By opportunity costs they mean the profit forgone when the utility transmits power generated by competitors rather than generating and transmitting the power itself. From the utility's point of view efficient component pricing is extremely attractive, particularly when there is a concern for the recovery of stranded costs.

In postal service the existence of stranded costs is less obvious because the costs take the form of stranded labor. The fact that government postal services usually are saddled with powerful labor unions in most cases means that workers are paid an above-market wage, labor practices are inefficient, and union-motivated inertia slows the adaption of new technologies and working practices. The pension liabilities faced by some postal services—notably in Germany, where liabilities were estimated to be 60 billion deutsche marks (approximately $40 billion)[4]—create a problem similar to that of stranded costs. Thus, in the face of private competition with lower labor costs, government postal services find their labor costs locked in, almost impossible to reduce.

An attempt might be made to recover such liabilities by means of efficient component pricing. But a pricing rule like that one would preserve the status quo and reward such inefficiencies and past errors.

Access Pricing

The pricing of access will be a major problem faced by government postal services with increased competition. The dilemma is this: The more a government postal service gives customers options to provide or procure some of the postal functions themselves, usually in exchange for discounts, the more the postal service faces the danger of stranded costs. Currently little progress has been made to solve this problem.

Access pricing in the postal service takes two principal forms: worksharing and downstream access. One example of worksharing is presorting materials at the business or location of origin. Another form would be placing bar codes on mail before it is sent to the post office. Postal services for several years have offered discounts in exchange for such worksharing. The U.S. Postal Service is in many respects a leader in the use of such discounts.

Downstream access developed in part out of the discounts for presorting. Presorters get an additional discount, for example, for transporting their presorted mail to the most appropriate postal facility. For example, a firm in Washington, D.C., might presort all barcoded advertising mail to be distributed in Baltimore, which is about 40 miles away. It then might ship bags of mail via its own trucks or hired trucks to a central post office in Baltimore. The U.S. Postal Service would handle only the local delivery of this mail in Baltimore. The progress in downstream access promises to increase the speed and reliability of not only letter delivery but also parcels and small packets.

The U.S. Postal Service has made more progress in downstream access than have the national post offices in most other countries. For example, the British post office, considered an innovator in many respects, has discounts for large-volume presort mailers but no access further downstream. New Zealand has some downstream access and Australia provides limited opportunities for downstream access but with average discounts of only 1 cent.

Competition or the Lack Thereof

It should not be too surprising that major progress has not yet been made on either the problem of labor costs or access in post offices worldwide as competition has been confined to specific areas, particularly parcels and courier service. In the United States the U.S. Postal Service is not the major provider in those services. Federal Express (FedEx) and United Parcel Service (UPS) are the clear leaders there. Most of the other national post offices do not face competitors as strong as those in the United States, although competition in parcel and courier service is growing in most places. Presumably those businesses do not benefit significantly from the economies of the local delivery network. There has also been some competition as a result of the widespread use of faxes and e-mail, which have had an impact on business-to-business mail. However, that has probably had a greater impact on courier service and has mostly simply increased the volume of communication by the addition of new media.

Since most national carriers enjoy monopolies over delivery of traditional first-class letters, there have been few major efficiency gains in this area. In the United States the monopoly is enforced by the Private Express Statutes. The major exception, which makes possible the operation of overnight delivery companies such as FedEx, allows delivery by private carrier of urgent communications as long as the price charged is at least $3.00 or twice as much as the first-class rate.[5] The U.S. Postal Service also controls the use of mailboxes.

In other countries post offices enjoy monopolies on mail below certain weight or money limits. The British post office, for example, has a monopoly on letters priced below one British pound. In Germany, Deutsche Post AG has a monopoly for up to 10 times the standard first-class rate. France and The Netherlands have weight limits up to 1 kg and 500 mg, respectively. Mailbox monopolies do not exist outside the Unite States. While Sweden and Finland currently maintain the only national post offices with no monopoly protection, the extent of the protection is declining where the limit is expressed in money terms as there seems to be little likelihood that the monopoly limits will be raised with inflation. Sweden Post in fact faces competition from CityMail, a small private operator that makes deliveries four days a week in Stockholm only. One of its customers is the British post office. That is a potentially significant development. It is usually in local delivery that government monopoly supporters claim that economies of scale exist and that only one large enterprise can operate on a cost-effective basis. However, the company is small, with around 80 million Swedish kronor ($10 million) in sales compared with 22 billion kronor ($2.9 billion) for Sweden Post. The latter recently has purchased 75 percent of the stock of the former but, after a reorganization, sold its shares.

Table 1
STRUCTURE OF POSTAL SERVICES,
15 INDUSTRIAL COUNTRIES

	1990	1994	1996
PLC	3	6	10
Public corporation	5	7	5
Public administration	7	2	0

Worldwide Postal Structures

National postal services might be classified in one of three categories:

- Public Limited Corporations (PLCs) are organized like any private corporation. They enjoy the freedom of private firms to manage their own affairs rather than suffer under the usually more restrictive rules that apply to government enterprises. They issue stock, though it is often owned by governments. They are mandated to seek profits. That gives them a greater incentive to seek efficient ways to operate.
- Public corporations have some of the flexibility of PLCs but are not supposed to seek profits. They do not issue stock.
- Public administration arrangements essentially are government-owned and -run operations like any other government agencies.

Joëlle Toledano of La Poste, the French postal service, believes that national carriers in 15 major industrialized countries all have moved away from public administration organizations. Table 1 shows that progress.[6]

The U.S. Postal Service currently is planning to reorganize along corporate lines. However, one might question whether it should be classified as a public corporation at this time or is still closer to a public administration organization. The purely internal reforms likely will not be as extensive as major changes in national carriers in other countries. Many European countries have incorporated their post offices as PLCs. New Zealand's, Sweden's, and Germany's post offices have become PLCs wholly owned by the government. The Dutch post office is part of a holding company, KPN, that also owns the telephone company. The government owns 70 percent of the stock and the rest is traded on the Amsterdam Stock Exchange. That is the closest any major postal service has come to privatization.

There seems little impetus to privatization in most countries. A key reason is that all postal services have major unfunded pension obligations, currently guaranteed by governments. Privatized services could be too heavily burdened by those obligations. In Germany, as mentioned above, the problem is particularly serious with obligations of 60 billion deutsche marks in pensions. The U.S. Postal Service has unfunded pension liabilities estimated as high as $27 billion. Recently in Britain, the mecca of privatization, the government did a U-turn and not only decided against privatization but also stated its intentions of restricting the post office's commercial freedoms.

Despite the apparent lack of progress in privatizing and reorganizing mail service along more competitive lines, there is evidence of some innovation and increase in efficiency in foreign post offices. New Zealand Post has managed to improve service quality, make significant profits, and provide one of the lowest rates for first-class mail among major post offices.[7] It is planning to cut postal rates. PTT Post, the Dutch post office, has become a strong competitor in international mail through remailing. Potentially this kind of competition is a promising way of reducing inefficiencies in the way terminal dues are set.

Implications for the Future of Postal Service

Because the theoretical development of access pricing is still being debated it is not surprising that the development of access charging in postal service is still in its early stages of development. If postal services are to become strong competitors in an increasingly competitive industry then a number of prescriptions would seem to follow. Efficiency component pricing is not the appropriate mechanism because of its protection of the status quo and its failure to encourage innovation. The practice of offering worksharing discounts is ripe for rethinking, because of the greater significance of access pricing and the introduction of automation. Prebarcoding in an automation age may have value to a post office, but presorting may be of much lower value. New discount structures will be required. This could include even offering discounts to single-piece barcoded mail, that is, mail going to individual customers. This could mean that the use of the mail could still be an effective means to pay bills in competition with alternatives such as electronic means.

For postal services to become more efficient and for competition to become more widespread, privatization would seem to be necessary. There is no substitute for market pressures and for customers with the option of switching to other service suppliers. For a public enterprise enjoying a mandated monopoly, such an incentive does not exist. Who after all is going to work hard just to benefit the Treasury? Under privatization the board of directors has the incentive to provide stock options and other bonuses to motivate top management, and top management has an incentive to motivate management and other employees. Although agency problems exist in large private companies, problems are likely to be greater in a public enterprise owing to the minimal incentives that operate in the enterprise efficiently. However desirable a move to privatization might be because of efficiency incentives, it would be opposed by unions and other interest groups.

The recent British experience, in which the union led a highly successful campaign against privatization, illustrates the importance of this point. There is little doubt that in the United States organized labor, with the backing of most of the 800,000 U.S. Postal Service workers, would oppose privatization. A privatized postal service, without monopoly protection, facing increased competition, would not be able to maintain existing wage levels and practices. It would reduce job security, use more part-time and casual employees, and lower wages and job security of regular employees. Other problems could arise from profit-oriented postal service competitors that might be able to cross-subsidize between the services they offer to remain competitive.

Solutions such as partial employee ownership might be a possible approach if the problem of unfunded pension liabilities were addressed. It would be very difficult to put together a coalition to bring about privatization of the U.S. Postal Service any time soon. Given this difficulty, are there any less radical policies that could be introduced?

While these are difficult problems to overcome, drawing on experiences in other countries, possibilities emerge:

1. Like that of European countries the U.S. Postal Service's status might change to that of a for-profit company with greater autonomy to manage its own labor and other policies, but with all or most stock owned by the federal government.

2. The regulation could be changed at the same time to a price cap model, for example, similar to that proposed by Crew and Kleindorfer, with the cap applying only to a restrictive range of monopoly services.[8]
3. The Private Express Statutes could be repealed and replaced by a simple monopoly limit, but private providers would be required to charge at least 1 dollar for any delivery.
4. Postal unions could be given normal rights to strike instead of the current arrangements of binding arbitration.

Some critics might find the changes limited and simple. However, they could have far-reaching effects. They would provide the opportunity to change the status of management and nonunion staff to increase the potential for bonuses and other incentives. They would encourage management to work out contracts with its unions similar to those of privately owned companies. If there is a lesson to be learned from experience in Europe and elsewhere in the world, it might be not to expect too much too quickly. The limited legal and regulatory changes provide an opportunity to lead events possibly in the direction of more radical change later.

Notes

1. Jeffrey M. Perloff and Michael L. Wachter, "A Comparative Analysis of Wage Premiums and Industrial Relations in the British Post Office and the United States Postal Service," in *Competition and Innovation in Postal Services*, ed. Michael A. Crew and Paul R. Kleindorfer (Boston: Kluwer Academic Publishers, 1991), p. 132. In view of data limitations and mixed results for the U.K., Wachter and Perloff qualify their estimates as tentative.

2. The postal unions recently played a major role in devaluing the British Government's proposals to privatize the Post Office.

3. William J. Baumol and J. Gregory Sidak, *Transmission Pricing and Stranded Costs in the Electric Power Industry* (Washington, D.C.: AEI Press, 1995), p. 178.

4. Frank Pieper and Stumpf Ulrich, "Restructuring the Postal Sector—the German Case," presented at the Rutgers University Conference on Postal and Delivery Services, Saltsjöbaden, Sweden, May 18–21, 1994, provided this figure based on an earlier paper by F. Arnold, "Managmentholding oder Beteiligungsholding?" in *Privatisierung der Telekom-Zielsetzung und Bedeutung für den Standort Deutschland*, eds. B. Bauer and Karl-Heinz Neumann, (Bad Honnef, 1994) pp. 43-55. Arnold (1994). The discussion is interesting for examining the problems to be faced in privatizing the German post office.

5. 39 CFR Sec. 320.6C.

6. Jölle Toledano, "Is There Any Common Trend in European Liberalization Strategies?" paper presented at Rutgers University Workshop on Postal Economics, Naantali, Finland, June 7–10, 1995.

7. For a detailed review of some of the developments in New Zealand Post see Elmar Toime, "Foreword: The Commercial Postal Businesses," in *Commercialization of Postal and Delivery Services: National and International Perspectives*, eds. Michael A. Crew and Paul R. Kleindorfer (Boston: Kluwer Academic Publishers, 1995).

8. Michael A. Crew and Paul K. Kleindorfer, "Pricing, Entry, and Innovation under a Commercialized Postal Service," in *Governing the Postal Service*, ed. J. Gregory Sidak (Washington, D.C.: AEI Press, 1994). The plan would allow the U.S. Postal Service automatically to raise its rates by the Consumer Price Index minus some "x" on its monopoly service for a period of five years. During that period the U.S. Postal Service would have an incentive to cut costs. The Postal Rate Commission would monitor the U.S. Postal Service to ensure that quality is maintained.

References

A Strategic Review of Progressive Postal Administrations. Report to the United States Postal Service by Price Waterhouse, February 1995.

William J. Baumol and J. Gregory Sidak, "The Pricing of Inputs Sold to Competitors," *Yale Journal on Regulation* (1994): 172–202.

"A Comparative Analysis of Wage Premiums and Industrial Relations in the British Post Office and the United States Postal Service," in *Competition and Innovation in Postal Services*, ed. Michael A. Crew and Paul R. Kleindorfer (Boston: Kluwer Academic Publishers, 1991).

101

10. Problems with Privatization

Murray Comarow

I was the executive director of a President's Commission on Postal Organization whose recommendations persuaded Congress, in 1970, to reorganize the old Post Office Department into the U.S. Postal Service (USPS). I later served as senior assistant postmaster general. Since then, on behalf of clients, I have followed its ups and downs for more than a quarter of a century.

I urge the appointment of another nonpartisan commission to analyze the causes of the Postal Service's problems, and recommend changes.

Current Conditions

Some will question the need for such a study, and they can make a plausible case that "it ain't broke." *U.S. News/CNN* reported, according to Postmaster General Marvin T. Runyon, that 87 percent of the public has a favorable opinion of the Postal Service. Delivery of first-class mail is at record levels, he says. The 32-cent stamp is the second cheapest among major nations. Japan's is 74¢, Germany's 59¢, Sweden's 36¢, Great Britain's 37¢.

Further, the USPS held the line on prices from January 1991 to January 1995 and is currently operating at a surplus. Postal costs are not borne by taxpayers. Customers, mostly businesses, pay the freight. Postal costs have gone up less than the rate of inflation.

With some 800,000 employees, the Postal Service delivered 177 billion pieces of mail in 1994 to 123 million addresses—more in one day than Federal Express delivers in a year, more in three days than United Parcel Service in a year, more than the eight next largest nations combined, 40 percent of the world's mail.

Since the 1970 reorganization, the Postal Service has been self-supporting. Political appointments of postmasters and other officials

The author is a distinguished adjunct professor at American University.

have been eliminated; in fact, they are unlawful. Thousands of good men and women have been promoted to jobs previously reserved for patronage appointments. Mail was delivered in the "good old days" before postal reform at great and hidden cost to the taxpayer. Congress simply appropriated whatever it took—up to 25 percent of postal costs—to keep the Post Office running despite its red ink. The 8¢ stamp was really 10¢.

Granted that postal reorganization has much to its credit, one must acknowledge the dark side:

- Billions of dollars invested in automation have resulted in little increase in productivity. The General Accounting Office (GAO) reported in June 1994 that the massive 1992 USPS reorganization and employee buyout program brought automation—the lifeblood of postal operations—to a virtual halt and created serious service problems. That buyout also violated the veterans preference laws.
- Contributing to service problems was a strange decision to bifurcate responsibility at field offices between operations managers and customer service managers.
- Another problem is sheer incompetence. Managers at Chicago and elsewhere, whose incompetence achieved unprecedented levels, were merely transferred at no loss of pay.
- The "remote barcoding program," at Binghamton, New York, once employed contract employees at about $7.50 an hour. The Postal Service decided to replace them with postal clerks at double the wage. The costs of that decision are huge. A total of 37,000 new barcoding jobs are being created at 10 centers.
- Employment today exceeds predownsizing levels in every worker category—career, casual, and transitional. There are 38,000 more postal employees now than three years ago.

But suppose the nation's dozen best executives could be persuaded to fill the top postal jobs. They would undoubtedly do a better job, but they would have a tough time. The reasons will be clearer if viewed against a bit of history.

Earlier Reforms

The President's Commission on Postal Organization, chaired by American Telephone and Telegraph's chairman Frederick R. Kappel, was appointed by President Lyndon B. Johnson on April 8, 1967. Its principal conclusion, identical to that of the 1949 Commission on Organization of the Executive Branch, chaired by former president Herbert Hoover, was this:

> Our basic finding is that the procedures for administering the ordinary executive departments of Government are inappropriate for the Post Office.

The two main alternatives rejected by the commission three decades ago were privatization and political management. The men who reached that conclusion included six CEOs of such companies as American Telephone and Telegraph, General Electric, and Bank of America; the dean of the Harvard Business School; two prominent Democrats; and the AFL-CIO's George Meany, although Meany never actually attended a meeting.

Here is what they said about privatization:

> Were the postal system being started today, it might well be operated by a privately owned regulated corporation. . . . We have concluded, however, that a transfer of the postal system to the private sector is not feasible, largely for reasons of financing; the Post Office should therefore continue under government ownership. The possibility remains of private ownership at some future time, if such a transfer were then considered to be feasible and in the public interest.

The reform proposal was strongly supported by Presidents Johnson and Nixon, and by both parties. In a remarkable display of unity, a citizens' committee to support postal reform was organized and cochaired by Larry O'Brien and Thurston Morton, chairmen of the Democratic and Republican parties, respectively. President Nixon's postmaster general, Winton M. Blount, lobbied effectively, promising that political appointments would cease. He kept his word.

The postal union's resistance to reform began to crack, and when the pot was sweetened with an 8 percent pay raise, and, against the Kappel Commission's advice, a promise of binding arbitration, they fell into line.

Congress accepted the Commission's recommendations with several changes. Two turned out to be critical:

- Congress established a politically appointed Postal Rate Commission, rather than having rates initially set, after full hearings, by a panel of three professional, nonpolitical administrative law judges.
- Congress required binding arbitration, rather than leaving it to the president to resolve any collective bargaining impasse.

Both changes have had severe consequences and will continue to burden the Postal Service regardless of its leadership.

The Issues and Players

A review of the various issues and players helps clarify the USPS's problems.

The Postal Rate Commission

The Postal Rate Commission is headed by five commissioners appointed by the president. Currently three of the five are former Senate staffers. Rate cases run as long as 10 months. A full case record in 1990 filled a 10-foot shelf. The decision alone ran almost 1,000 pages. Between rate cases, which come along every three or four years, the commissioners and their 50-person staff do things that many believe intrude on postal management. The Postal Rate Commission is the only government agency whose job it is to set prices for another government entity. The character and integrity of the Rate Commission men and women is not in question; its role in the scheme of things is.

Binding Arbitration

This is part of the price Congress paid for union support. It has been a boon for postal unions and a disaster for postal customers. The USPS is labor intensive: the General Accounting Office reported recently that 81.7 percent of its costs go for wages and fringe benefits. Incredibly, this situation has not changed since 1970. (The Postal Service claims that it is down to 80 percent.) Billions of dollars invested in automation have had little effect on efficiency. The average postal clerk or carrier earns $34,600 a year. Including retirement and health costs, that comes to over $44,000 a year, without overtime. State and local employees who do similar work make $10,000 a year less. Private-sector employees doing similar work are even less well paid.

The root of the pay problem is Section 101(c) of the Postal Reorganization Act of 1970. It commands that the USPS set employee pay "comparable to the rates and types of compensation paid in the private sector." In the first round of collective bargaining in the early 1970s, weak-kneed postal executives, largely recruited from industry, acceded to union demands that "comparable" meant other highly unionized industries, rather than similar work in the private sector at large. Also won by the unions were cost-of-living increases, no-layoff provisions, and incredibly complex work rules.

The Kappel Commission had recommended that the Federal Mediation and Conciliation Service try to settle contract questions or pay disputes; if mediation failed, binding arbitration could be used only if both parties agreed. Otherwise the issue would be referred to the President, who would employ whatever methods he chose to resolve the matter. The Commission's report said: "The uncertainties for both parties built into the final stages of this procedure make for more meaningful bargaining and are, in our view, a source of strength."

If binding arbitration is too deeply embedded to eliminate, a variation known as "final offer arbitration" should be considered. Basically, each party places its "final offer" on the table—the whole package, or issue by issue. The arbitrator chooses one. A party's position on an issue must be reasonable if it is to stand a chance of being selected. That places more responsibility on the shoulders of the parties, where it belongs, and less on an arbitrator.

The White House and the Board of Governors

The 1971 law states that "the Postal Service shall be directed by a Board of Governors composed of 11 members." Nine are appointed by the president. The nine select a postmaster general and deputy, who become board members. Of the nine, not more than five may be of the same political party, and the statute wisely mandates that they shall "represent the public interest generally," not "specific interests using the Postal Service."

Meeting two days a month, the governors deserve the nation's gratitude for years of service at a pay level, $10,000 annually, which is an anachronistic insult. But directing the affairs of a huge enterprise is not just a matter of common sense. Governors inexperienced in major corporate activities cannot contribute insights into running large companies and make mistakes in selecting postmasters general.

Indeed, of the eight postmasters general hired by the governors, only a couple were well regarded by the cognizant business community. The finger points directly at the White House, from President Nixon to President Clinton. The organizing principle of postal reform was to get rid of political management and permit the Postal Service to operate in a businesslike way. That requires the appointment of governors and postmasters general who know how to do that. Perhaps the president should look to an objective panel, similar to the American Bar Association's evaluation of candidates for the federal bench.

The Congress

While mandating that the Postal Service function efficiently and in a businesslike way, Congress erected barriers to doing so, over and above the binding arbitration and rate-setting barriers. Section 101(b) of the Postal Reorganization Act states that "[no] small post office shall be closed solely for operating at a deficit. . . ." William I. Henderson, the Postal Service's chief operating officer, says that 26,000 small post offices out of about 40,000 offices cost over $4 for every $1 they take in, and that other ways are available for good, even better, service.

Congressional resistance is often encountered when postal management undertakes money-making activities. If management is to manage, it must be free to innovate. This is especially true with respect to experimental and competitive postal rates, which are exceedingly difficult to set under existing law. Postal Rate Commission approval for competitive rates can take many months.

The Postal Monopoly and "Privatization"

The most compelling task of a new presidential commission may well be to revisit the Private Express Statutes that created a postal monopoly on letters and addressed advertising mail. All other delivery functions—parcels, magazines and newspapers, and the like—have long been competitive. The monopoly, which goes back to the Continental Congress, is based on a congressional policy decision to deliver letters at a uniform rate to the entire nation. How important is that today? Conservative economists Michael A. Crew of Rutgers University and Paul R. Kleindorfer of the Wharton School of Finance favor commercializing the USPS, yet argue that "universal service must continue to be available to all citizens as a basic ingredient of the modern nation state."[1] Permitting competition would open the door to "cream skimming," said Postal Rate Commission Chairman Edward J. Gleiman recently, arguing that entrepreneurs would eagerly deliver mail in profitable areas, but would leave to the Postal Service the Hawaii to Alaska mail, or service in high-crime urban areas.

In remarks in May 1995 to a Direct Marketing Association conference, Chairman John M. McHugh, House Postal Affairs Subcommittee, said that he was sensitive to the postal needs of rural Americans, adding that privatization proponents would have to demonstrate how they would improve service and keep costs in check. He referred to privatization, in fact, as a "threat."

A case study in the clash between ideology and reality is Illinois Republican Rep. Phil Crane's bill, H.R. 210, strongly supported by California Republican Rep. Dana Rohrabacher. Mr. Crane has introduced the same bill for years. Its purpose: "To provide for the privatization of the Postal Service." Section 2(a) of that bill says, however, that the private corporation must guarantee the "delivery of postal services in a manner consistent with section 101(b) of title 39, United States Code." As mentioned above, section 101(b) provides "No small post office shall be closed solely for operating at a deficit, it being the specific intent of the Congress that effective postal services be insured to residents of both urban and rural communities." Is that "privatization?"

Ideological arguments about privatization tend to founder on the underlying details—except that they are not, of course, details at all. They constitute public policy/economic issues that need patient analysis. Here are some of them:

- Should there be a board of governors; if so, how do we get the right people on it?
- Is there any way to restrict Congress from micromanagement and from using postal customers' money for nonpostal purposes?
- How should rates be set?
- How should wages be set?
- Should postal employees have the right to strike? If so, should postal management have the right of lockout or the right to hire permanent replacement workers?
- Should the Postal Service be permitted to bid against competitors like Federal Express and United Parcel Service for major contracts?

- Should the letter-mail monopoly be terminated; if so, would other deliverers have access to mailboxes?
- Should the Postal Service be authorized to close unprofitable outlets?
- Should it cost more to send a letter to distant areas?
- Finally, should the Postal Service become a private corporation? If so, how would mail be forwarded for the 40 million Americans who move each year? Who would assume the responsibilities of the Postal Inspection Service? The FBI? Local police?

The Mailers Council is a coalition of the Postal Service's biggest customers. It accounts for 76 percent of the mail. A recent Harris poll commissioned by the council revealed this about their own members:

- Three of four agree that the Postal Service "is the best way to provide mail delivery for everyone at a reasonable price."
- AT&T-style deregulation as a model for reforming the USPS was not favored by most of the very largest mailers, but was favored by a majority of other mailers.
- 96 percent favor more contracting out with private companies.

I would eliminate the Postal Rate Commission and the requirements for binding arbitration. Small, unprofitable post offices should be closed, provided that service could be maintained, and it could, especially by placing postal facilities in local businesses or by using rural carriers. The Postal Service should be able to compete for large contracts and to offer experimental services.

For the present, however, I would maintain the monopoly on first-class letters, as well as nationwide service at uniform prices, but those issues certainly should be on the table. Nor would I give postal unions the right to strike, a "right" possessed by no other federal employees.

That still leaves the question of privatization. Postal reform was essential but does not meet today's needs. The president, Congress, the mailing community, and the Postal Service itself must recognize that the experience of the past 25 years warrants a new and far-ranging study. This proposal is consistent with Republican interest in greater efficiency and Democratic initiatives for "reinventing government." The nation needs and has a right to a better designed, better run postal service.

I am deeply concerned, however, with the prospect of ill-considered action taken under the banner of privatization or its cousins: commercialization, corporatization, deregulation, and devolution. A theological conviction that privatization will reduce rates and improve service is not persuasive. As Eric Sevareid famously remarked, "The chief cause of problems is solutions."

Note

1. American Enterprise Book Summary, undated, received December 1994.

PART IV

PRIVATIZATION PLANS

11. Employee Ownership of the Postal Service

Rep. Dana Rohrabacher

Despite increases in stamp prices, management reorganization, and other reforms, the quality of postal service continues to decline. The problems do not rest on the shoulders of postal employees. The plight of the U.S. Postal Service (USPS) can be blamed on the bureaucratic and monopoly structure imposed by the federal government.

To bring about lower prices and better service, the government should begin to empower postal workers with the rights and responsibilities of ownership. In other words, the government should turn the Postal Service into the world's largest employee-owned company through an Employee Stock Ownership Plan (ESOP).

I am an original cosponsor of Congressman Phil Crane's bill H.R. 210, which will turn the employees of the Postal Service into the owners of the Postal Service. In return, Americans will enjoy better postal service while the employees will experience a better working environment.

The Problem

Mail delivery is 15 percent slower than it was 25 years ago. Customers face inconvenient post office hours, decreasing worker productivity, poor customer service, and truckloads of undelivered mail. Those are just a few of the problems facing the Postal Service as well. Despite a continuing decrease in quality service, the USPS implemented a postal rate increase on January 1, 1995. What will the extra money consumers must spend on postage pay for—better service? Don't kid yourself!

The author is a Republican member of the U.S. House of Representatives from the 45th District of California.

The federal government originally established the post office in the 1780s as a means of keeping in contact with remote areas of the still-developing United States. At that time, there was no other communication network in place. Today we have an entirely different story. Telephones, facsimile machines, cable, satellites, computers, television, and radio are all methods used by people to communicate. Businesses are abandoning the USPS in favor of the information superhighway. As a result, mail delivery is now just another nonessential service provided by the federal government and is no longer the sole essential communication network. As the level of service provided by the Postal Service continues to decline and postal rates continue to rise, more consumers are turning toward alternative communication methods such as those previously mentioned.

For too long, American consumers have been denied efficient service and reasonable postal rates as a result of the Postal Service monopoly. Blame should not rest with hard-working, tax-paying postal employees. The blame, instead, should rest with a protected USPS system that perpetuates inefficiency and nonresponsiveness to consumers. In an effort to improve the efficiency of the USPS, various solutions, from new management styles to complete reorganization, have been tried, to no avail. It is obvious that a major change is necessary to keep the USPS afloat.

The Solution

The most effective means to improve the responsiveness of the USPS is competition. Competition gives managers and workers the incentive to provide satisfactory customer service at a reasonable price. Employees understand that their jobs depend on customer satisfaction. Without competition, employees have few incentives to provide exceptional service, and the USPS lacks incentives to control costs and maintain high quality.

In an era of massive federal deficits, privatization represents an effective means toward reducing the scope of government spending while providing Americans with more effective services. Employee ownership may well be a useful method of privatization. Today, unions and government employees, for the most part, vigorously oppose privatization. Often the sticking point is workers' apprehension about the possible loss of retirement and pension funds. If privatization schemes work toward both guaranteeing the current pensions for present employees and empowering those employees with the ownership of a major business enterprise—capital assets and all—privatization becomes a good deal more palatable to those on the federal payroll. Government workers in such a scenario may well be inclined to become employee owners of private, taxpaying enterprises.

Employee Stock Ownership Plans

Economic freedom and individual ownership are prerequisites for political liberty and human progress. What we do to expand ownership and broaden the base of participation in our free enterprise system will bolster the underpinnings of American democracy and strengthen the economic foundation that has supported our country's unparalleled prosperity. Free enterprise, our engine of progress, is dependent on a general acceptance of and respect for property rights. By expanding private ownership of both property and capital, we can broaden and secure the base of freedom while bolstering economic growth. ESOPs are effective tools in achieving that goal.

Employee owners approach their jobs with a far different attitude than most working people. They feel personally responsible for their company's performance, they are loyal to their company, and they are responsive to its needs. That situation, in turn, creates a productive sense of teamwork between management and nonmanagerial employees. Increasing the level of employee ownership will help make America a richer, more competitive country by empowering working people with the rights and responsibilities of ownership, giving them incentives they never had as hourly employees.

The Plan Explained

The ESOP is a financing tool that serves as an incentive for companies and corporations to structure their finances so that employees gain an ownership stake in the company for which they work. When properly designed and implemented, the ESOP is a capital credit device that uses a corporation's credit and future profits to enable employees to buy a sizable ownership share in the company. This is often done in conjunction with asset acquisition and corporate expansion.

117

The ESOP channels capital credit to corporations through an employee trust. The loans are subject to the same prudent standards and corporate guarantees as are direct loans. The loan funds are then used to purchase stock for the workers. The loan itself is repaid with corporate earnings. The ESOP allocates stock to the accounts of individual employees as a block of shares "earned"—that is, the company contributes cash from pretax profits to the trust. The cash, which is treated as a tax-deductible employee benefit, is used to repay the stock acquisition loan. Traditional corporate leverage credit aids the existing owners of the company. The ESOP uses a corporation's credit to convert its workers into owners.

H.R. 210: Creating the World's Largest ESOP

Although many federal agencies would be good candidates for privatization, the USPS remains the most visible. H.R. 210 would achieve this goal with the following steps:

> **1.** It would transfer, in its entirety, the USPS, including all assets, liabilities, and net worth to some 800,000 postal employees, making it the largest employee-owned company in the world, and giving those employees a real incentive to contribute to increased productivity. Assets include thousands of parcels of real estate properties across the country currently owned by the USPS. Most of this property is underutilized and could be sold off with profits going to the new worker-owners. The value of stock provided to each employee will be in the tens of thousands of dollars.
> **2.** The bill would guarantee that retirement benefits provided to employees of the new employee-owned postal service must be comparable with those that would have been afforded to those individuals as employees of the Postal Service had this bill not been enacted. The new company would be responsible for the retirement provisions for any employees hired thereafter.
> **3.** The bill would give the new Postal Service ESOP a five-year grace period before allowing competition by repealing the Private Express Statutes. USPS already contracts with private companies for 10 percent of its business operations, and competes with Federal Express, United Parcel Service, and others for urgent and overnight service.
> **4.** The bill would provide incentives for restructuring and modernizing the antiquated and inefficient Postal Service,

and hence would vastly improve one of the fundamental services on which every American depends.

5. The bill would enhance the federal, state, and local tax base with increased productivity and privatization, placing Postal Service income and property on the tax rolls for the first time.

6. The bill would provide long-term protection for taxpayers by removing the economic liability of this government's single largest nonmilitary enterprise.

In conclusion, employee ownership would bring higher quality service at competitive rates to this nation's postal customers. And privatization via ESOP would empower postal employees with the means to control their own future, and would bring to play all the incentives and profit motives inherent in the competitive free enterprise system. With privatization, postal employees could find themselves profiting directly from working more efficiently.

12. Breaking Up the Postal Monopoly

Douglas K. Adie

In 1988 the Cato Institute held a conference on privatizing the U.S. Postal Service (USPS). At that conference then–Postmaster General Anthony Frank said,

> Throwing out the private express statutes, thereby eliminating the letter-mail monopoly,. . . I am against it, because I believe the U.S. Postal Service is a legitimate and necessary *public* institution that serves an important social function as a binding, unifying force in our national life.[1]

In addition to the usual litany of "natural monopoly," "cream-skimming," and "social mission" arguments for preserving the postal monopoly, Frank maintained that "the mail system, like Humpty Dumpty, once broken, couldn't be put back together again." And not unexpectedly, he enumerated the various means the Postal Service would use to be improve its efficiency.

Nearly eight years later the Postal Service has faced new scandals over lost mail, slow deliveries, and increased prices for stamps. The current postmaster general, Marvin T. Runyon, is attempting to reform the Postal Service and promises efficiency improvements. But the broken record of promise and failure can continue only as long as the USPS enjoys monopoly protection from competition. The question is not whether it should be privatized, but how?

One approach would be simply to give or sell the USPS as a unit to its workers, or to sell it to the general public and interested businesses, while removing its monopoly protection. But allowing the Postal Service to remain a single unit would leave too powerful an entity that still could crush competitors. And if the postal workers are given the Postal Service to purchase their support or at least

The author is a professor of economics in the Department of Economics at Ohio University in Athens, Ohio, and author of *Monopoly Mail*, published by the Cato Institute.

acquiescence in the privatization plan, the taxpayers will be the big losers.

The Humpty Dumpty approach feared by Frank should be embraced. The best way to privatize the Postal Service would be to break it up into five regional divisions, similar to the way American Telephone and Telegraph's (AT&T's) local telephone operations were made into independent regional systems. In that way true markets could be established by mail delivery.

Preliminaries to Privatization

The Cato Institute conference of eight years ago confirmed the need to privatize the Postal Service; suggestions from that conference can provide guidelines for the effort. Peter Ferrara in his introduction to *Free the Mail*,[2] the collection of conference papers, divided privatization into a useful sequence of discrete steps. The timetable for the states could be increased or reduced as needed. The sequence, with minor revisions, follows:

1. Eliminate the Postal Service's right of eminent domain;
2. Repeal the mail monopoly for third-class advertisements;
3. Remove restrictions on the use of addressees' mailboxes by competitors;
4. Eliminate government subsidies for employee pension retirement and health benefits;
5. Eliminate government subsidies and mandates for reduced rate for charities and congressional franking privileges;
6. Terminate the Postal Service's right to use federal institutions to borrow, and remove the Treasury guarantee of Postal Service debt instruments;
7. Revoke the Postal Rate Commission's authority over rates for second-, third-, and fourth-class mail;
8. Finally, permit private firms to deliver first-class mail: first, within and into rural areas; second, between business firms; and third, the remaining first-class mail.

Ideally, postal deregulation and privatization should proceed on a bipartisan basis. After all, it was Sen. Edward M. Kennedy, the Massachusetts Democrat, assisted by Stephen Breyer, President Clinton's recent Supreme Court appointee, who led the way in airline deregulation, and Rep. John Dingell, the Michigan Democrat, who was instrumental in the privatization of Conrail. But the 800,000 unionized postal workers likely will make the bipartisan approach difficult.

Two questions then remain to be addressed:

- First, should the USPS, with its 800,000 workers, $55 billion per year budget, and presence in every part of the country, be sold as a unit or should it be broken up first and sold in parts as separate companies?
- And second, who should receive the benefits from the sale—that is, should the Postal Service be given to the postal employees in an Employee Stock Ownership Plan, or should it be sold in regular stock offerings to all interested bidders, with proceeds helping reduce the deficit, or for a cash dividend?

There is no clear reason why the Postal Service must remain a unitary system to operate efficiently. An elaborate private disaggregated check-clearing system in this country, for example, moves checks around quickly and cheaply, and bypasses the Federal Reserve system.

The protection afforded the Postal Service by its monopoly status, and the Service's national reach and overall size, make it difficult to privatize. Its 800,000-person labor force represents more than .6 percent of the country's 130-million civilian labor force. Its annual budget of $55 billion is around .8 percent of the United States's gross domestic product. Its continued existence as a unitary privatized corporation would allow it to retain too much power and influence. Further, its importance could tempt a future Congress to give it aid as an "essential" industry or even to nationalize it again.

The best approach to privatization then would be to break the USPS up first and sell it off gradually one division at a time, to allow the market to digest the stock offerings. The stock should be sold to any and all bidders. Perhaps some price reduction for stock purchases might be given to postal employees and managers to ensure their cooperation and to provide them an incentive to work constructively and efficiently. The proceeds of such a stock offering should be used primarily to reimburse taxpayers who are the rightful owners of this public corporation.

The AT&T Model

The founding father of AT&T, Theodore Vail, applied the rhetoric of the early Post Office to the telephone. He called for a system that was interdependent, affording the opportunity for any subscriber on any exchange to communicate with any other subscriber on any other exchange. He envisioned a telephone system "as universal and extensive as the highway system of the country which extends from every man's door to every other man's door." Vail, like many in the Postal Service, did not believe that universal service could be "accomplished by separately controlled or distinct systems."[3]

The experience since the breakup of AT&T demonstrates that Vail was wrong. His vision had appeal, but he lacked understanding of the way market forces can provide coordination and freedom at the same time.

Breaking up the Postal Service would not eliminate efficiencies realized from common ownership and control of postal services. The reason is that such efficiencies do not exist. Vertically integrated services in the USPS include collection, sorting, bulk transportation of mail between cities, and delivery. But such services do not gain efficiency because they are coordinated by a central authority. Mail flows would not be chaotic in a competitive environment. Coordination does not necessarily result from common ownership and control. More effective coordination can result from each independent service provider realizing it can profit from becoming more compatible with other providers. AT&T's economists said there would be huge coordination problems when the company's local operations were divested. But that did not happen.

Unitary Problem

The unitary nature and central planning of the Postal Service creates its own coordination problems similar to those of a socialist state. Business owners in competition with one another to provide goods and services both generate and use knowledge concerning market demand. Although each entrepreneur discovers only bits of knowledge, the spontaneous interaction of bidders in the market brings prices into relation with costs, allocates resources efficiently, and maximizes welfare.

Smaller businesses can use price and profit-and-loss information to forecast where costs should be cut; what the profit-maximizing uses and prices of raw materials, equipment, labor, and other inputs are; and what mix of goods and services will best satisfy consumers.

124

The managers of the Postal Service have inherent problems making such determinations. This is not because individual entrepreneurs are smarter than managers of larger businesses. Rather, it is because the USPS, thanks to its monopoly, encompasses most of the document delivery market. All of its participants are on the same team and the competitive process is nonexistent.

If the Postal Service remains a unitary system, it will have the capacity, even if privatized, to erect barriers to the entry of new firms. Anti-competitive practices would include the following:

- Using legal details and processes to increase the cost of entry for competitors. For example, it could file frivolous lawsuits and, with more money to pay lawyers, outlast smaller competitors in drawn-out cases;
- Deterring the entry of competitors by precommitting investment funds for areas far in advance of expenditures. It could anticipate where smaller firms were planning to make investments and scare off those investors with its own capital muscle;
- Charging exorbitant fees to independent delivery systems to interconnect with it, then charge high rates for each unit of mail that it handles from an independent delivery system;
- Using exclusionary pricing policies to cultivate the business of large patrons;
- Using predatory pricing in areas where small independent delivery systems operate.

A series of regional postal companies would be less likely then a large unitary company to engage in such anti-competitive practices.

Examples of the likely problems with a private but unitary Postal Service can be found in the private but unitary AT&T before its breakup. AT&T became too large, pervasive, and powerful for state or federal agencies to regulate. This is not to say that a private USPS should be regulated. It is to suggest that it would be difficult for anyone to make necessary business determinations about a unitary enterprise that dominates a sector of the economy.

For instance, the Federal Trade Commission was unable to measure AT&T's costs and so could not determine its interstate rates or the terms of access to local facilities. Many of the same problems of discovery of information are present in the mail service industry where the Postal Service dominates. In the telecommunications industry before the breakup, knowledge and information expanded so rapidly they could not be assembled, contained, and utilized within AT&T. Also, despite the fact that AT&T was a profit-making business, there was not sufficient motivation to introduce existing technology as rapidly as it was developing. Instead, planning within AT&T became devoted to the preservation of systems and equipment already in use, a practice that retarded innovations. Much of this description applies with equal force to the Postal Service under existing circumstances.

Divestiture Strategy

The Postal Service should be divided into seven divisions. Five would be the actual regional Postal Operating Companies (POCs). One would be a parcel post company. And one might eventually provide support services to coordinate operations between regional companies. But this last division's important initial task would be to serve as a holding company for the other POCs and the parcel service until they are sold. The company could be called the U.S. Postal Service Investment Corporation. It could assign assets and personnel and appoint management and temporary boards of directors.

It might also be advisable during the transition to allow the POCs to accumulate surpluses and profits as if they already were private. That would prepare them to operate competitively in the private sector.

Of course, repealing the private express statues that maintain the current postal monopoly is the essence of any privatization plan. That might be done, on a region-by-region basis, concurrently with the sale to the private sector of each POC.

The question might be raised whether five is the optimal number of regional companies. Eugene B. Dalton, president of the National League of Postmasters, said in a slightly different context, "If I were Postmaster General ... the first thing I would do is reestablish at least 10 regions versus 5, do away with three levels of management and save money."[4]

But the objective of structuring first and foremost should be divestiture of the U.S. Postal Service in the form of the POCs. No doubt, after divestiture, introduction of new equipment, development of new technology and, of course, competition from other suppliers will further restructuring on a voluntary basis, through mergers, acquisitions, and sales of companies.

Labor Changes

One of the benefits of the breakup and divestiture of the USPS is that it would simplify labor problems. Instead of having to deal with all workers represented together, each of the regional companies would conduct its own labor relations with its own employees and their representatives. Different regional companies may or may not be represented by unions. Some of the POCs might be able to reduce the scope of collective bargaining within their units. Work stoppages in one region need not affect services in any of the others. Strikes would not necessarily be catastrophic; they would merely give competitive local companies an opportunity to increase their market shares.

Up to the present the labor struggles in the Postal Service have not been very intense, but they have not been without cost. To avoid conflict, management has capitulated to many union demands. There has been little incentive for it to do otherwise. Giving in only required raising first-class postage a few cents. And low elasticity of demand did not reduce mail volume much.

Under the privatized postal system, unions, where they exist, will have the right to strike and will be covered by the same National Labor Relations Board rules that apply to all other private companies. Employers will have more freedom to negotiate and will negotiate only for their own companies. The important difference will be that management will have an incentive to negotiate diligently because the residual profit can be appropriated.

Abolition of the no-strike proviso under the privatized postal service should not spell disaster for the delivery of written communications because of competition generated by the repeal of the private express statutes. Both unions and management in each company will have a strong incentive to avoid strikes, work stoppages, or slowdowns lest customers shift their patronage to competing document delivery carriers.

Who Should Benefit from Privatization?

Over the past 20 years Rep. Philip M. Crane, the Illinois Republican, regularly has introduced legislation "to end the postal monopoly and permit competition." Now with the support of Rep. Dana

Rohrabacher, the California Republican, the plan would give the taxpayers' assets within the Postal Service to a corporation owned by the employees under an Employee Stock Ownership Plan. That would be a means to purchase the acquiescence of workers in privatization. But the plan hardly seems fair. Postal workers have extracted high salaries and subsidies from patrons and taxpayers over the years with their postal monopoly. They should not be rewarded further for that "success." The assets of the Postal Service belong to the taxpayers, who deserve to receive full value for them.

Who then might purchase the Postal Service? Certainly provision could be made to allow purchase of some portion of shares by parties who currently have an interest in the existing operation, such as employees, unions, or contractors. But purchase also should be open to private individuals, companies, or corporations who might tender an offer or bid at auction; and to the investing public through an issue of stock.

The Value of Postal Assets

How does one determine the amount of proceeds that the U.S. Postal Service Investment Corporation can realistically expect to realize through privatization? The earnings potential would be an important consideration that will limit the upper bound of what the government can hope to get for the Postal Service. As a lower bound it is important to know the liquidation value of the Postal Service's assets. That can be estimated by evaluating at market value all assets on the balance sheet for each division of the USPS to be privatized. Postal Service property and assets for each division need to be inventoried completely and evaluated at market prices. The inventory list should include: all property owned by the Postal Service, such as land, buildings, service locations, leasehold property; easement options, mineral reserves, water, and forestry land and timber; operational property such as power stations, warehouses, machinery, mobile equipment, rolling stock, fixtures, and fittings; and nonoperational properties, including investments. The inventory must include liabilities, most importantly, the unfunded pensions currently backed by the federal government.

The Postal Service is not at present a profit-making business, even with its nontaxed, monopoly status and the favorable borrowing rate it pays on the government-guaranteed bonds it issues. The law restricts it from earning a profit. More important, the Postal Service also has no incentive to do so because it is not possible legally to appropriate the profit. The incentive and motivation systems within the Postal Service do not adequately reward employees and managers for improving the efficiency of their operations.

There would be, however, tremendous opportunity for making profits in the Postal Service if it were privatized. Under current regulations, if revenues remained the same, costs could possibly be reduced by 50 percent.[5] To do this, one could cut the current wage rates of postal workers by at least one-third without impeding the ability to staff positions, and save over one-third of labor costs because postal workers are overpaid by that amount. Because labor costs are more than 85 percent of total costs, that alone would result in a cut in total costs of 28 percent. Also, automation, reorganization of functions, liberalization of work rules, and introduction of incentive systems into the wage and salary scales, instead of the severe compression that now exists, offer many opportunities for cutting costs. A merit system rather than a seniority system would provide more incentive for efficiency. Adoption of all the other cost-saving techniques, whether automation or the more efficient utilization of labor, should produce savings of at least another 22 percent, to make total savings of 50 percent feasible.

The Postal Service is inefficient now and still manages, on occasion, to break even. Although it enjoys special benefits now, the Postal Service has remarkable promise to be profitable if privatized under the best arrangement. Repealing the private express statutes is critical for assessing the USPS's profit potential because it would permit any firm to compete with the privatized postal service for any aspect of its business.

Conclusion

Postal Service privatization could introduce into the mail delivery business the kind of efficiency and integration now found in the telecommunications sector, with competitors introducing new services to customers, at lower prices. But that can occur only with real competition.

Selling off the U.S. Postal Service as a unit would allow it to block the dynamics of the market. And giving it to employees would simply reward those who already extract monopoly rents from customers and would cheat the taxpayers out of the benefits of their unfortunately forced investment.

The Postal Service then should be broken up into competing companies to ensure that true competition results.

Notes

1. Anthony M. Frank, "Efficiency, Yes; Balkanization, No," in Peter J. Ferrara, ed., *Free the Mail: Ending the Postal Monopoly* (Washington, D.C.: Cato Institute, 1990), p. 47.

2. Peter J. Ferrara, ed. *Free the Mail: Ending the Postal Monopoly* (Washington, D.C.: Cato Institute, 1990).

3. From Harry M. Shoogham III, ed., *Disconnecting Bell: The Impact of the AT&T Divestiture* (New York: Pergamon Press, 1984), p. 10. Taken from AT&T's 1910 annual report.

4. U.S. Congress, House of Representatives, Committee on Post Office and Civil Service, Subcommittee on Postal Operations and Service, *The Postal Service Act of 1979: Joint Hearings on H.R. 79*, 96th Cong., 1st sess., held March 6–22, p. 117.

5. See Madson Pirie, *Dismantling the State* (Dallas, Tex.: National Center for Policy Analysis, 1985), pp. 8–53. Pirie says that costs of production (in U.S. private industry) are 40 percent lower than in the public sector. Further, when provision for government services are contracted out, savings range from 20 percent to 40 percent. Further, postal workers are overpaid by about one-third. These figures suggest that a 50 percent savings from privatization is not unreasonable.

Index

INDEX

IBM, 60
Incorporation, of U.S. Postal Service, 4, 38–39, 110, 123
Industrial Revolution, 12, 53, 55
Information filters, 60
Information overload, 60
Information-processing systems. *See* Telecommunications
Information Revolution, 53–56, 60–61
Insurance documents, private carriage of, postal monopoly prohibition of, 17–18
Intercity transport service, early forms of, 11–14
International perspectives, on postal service competition, xi, 91–101
Internet, ix, xvi, xxiii–xxiv, 27, 35, 53, 55, 57–58, 61, 73

Jarrell, Gregg A., 69, 75
Johnson, Lyndon B., 105
Junction reports, 16

Kappel, Frederick R., 104–5, 107
Kennedy, Edward M., 122
Kleindorfer, Paul K., 100–101, 108
Koons, J. C., 22
KPN, 97

Labor changes, and postal reform, 127, 129
Labor costs, of postal service, xvii, 81, 91–93, 103–4, 106, 123
Lamar, William H., 17–18, 20
La Poste, 97
Large-scale production, competitive benefits of, 65–66
Large-volume mailers. *See* Mass mailers
Laughlin, James L., 65, 74
Legal monopoly, 27, 30
Lenard, Thomas M., ix, 24, 32, 52
Letter-box restrictions, 49
Letter carriers, early, 14
Letter monopoly, 44, 46–47, 49, 79, 110, 122
Letter postage, introduction of, 14
Letters
  obscene, mailability of, 17
  official definition of, 11, 14–21
  personal, as percentage of total mail, 80
Letter-sorting bureaus, private, for presorted mail, 24
Letter writing, versus instantaneous communication, 57, 79

Lewyn, Mark, xxv
Logo copyright infringement, xxii
Lotus Corporation, 60
LotusNotes, 60

MacVeagh, Wayne, 15, 20
Mail
  undelivered, 25–26
  volume of, 103
Mailable matter, definition of, 13
Mail Boxes, Etc., xix
Mail classification
  history of, 14
  reform case involving, 5
Mail delivery
  speed of, 25, 83–88
  tests of, 25
Mailers Council, 6, 110
Mail flows, structure of, 80, 124
Management
  postal, 4–5, 33, 109, 124–26
  political appointment of, 103–8
  of private companies, 44–45, 87
Market contracting, versus vertical integration, 82, 85–89, 124
Marketing, 28
Market structures, for private delivery, x–xii
Maryland, utility regulation in, 67–70
Mass broadcasting, 57–58
Mass mailers. *See also* Advertising mail, discounts for, xviii, 6, 95, 98
  in free market, 31
  problems of, viii–ix, 33–40, 46–48, 58
Mass paper transport, need for, 57, 59, 61
McAllister, Bill, xxv
McCormick, Christopher, 6
McGonegal, Stephen, 46, 52
McHugh, John M., 109
Meany, George, 105
Media, 57–58
Merline, John, xxv
Messenger system, lawfulness of, 17
Michaels, Robert, 72
Microprocessor, invention of, 54–55
Miller, James, 28
Miscellaneous matter, definition of, 14–15
Mises, Ludwig von, 66
Monopoly. *See* Legal monopoly; Natural monopoly; Postal monopoly
Morton, Thruston, 105
Mosaic, 58

134

About the Editor

Edward L. Hudgins is director of regulatory studies at the Cato Institute in Washington and senior editor of *Regulation* magazine. He previously was a senior economist at the Joint Economic Committee of the U.S. Congress, working for now–Majority Leader Dick Armey, and also served as director of the Center for International Economic Growth at the Heritage Foundation. Hudgins has a Ph.D. in political philosophy from the Catholic University of America.

Cato Institute

Founded in 1977, the Cato Institute is a public policy research foundation dedicated to broadening the parameters of policy debate to allow consideration of more options that are consistent with the traditional American principles of limited government, individual liberty, and peace. To that end, the Institute strives to achieve greater involvement of the intelligent, concerned lay public in questions of policy and the proper role of government.

The Institute is named for *Cato's Letters*, libertarian pamphlets that were widely read in the American Colonies in the early 18th century and played a major role in laying the philosophical foundation for the American Revolution.

Despite the achievement of the nation's Founders, today virtually no aspect of life is free from government encroachment. A pervasive intolerance for individual rights is shown by government's arbitrary intrusions into private economic transactions and its disregard for civil liberties.

To counter that trend, the Cato Institute undertakes an extensive publications program that addresses the complete spectrum of policy issues. Books, monographs, and shorter studies are commissioned to examine the federal budget, Social Security, regulation, military spending, international trade, and myriad other issues. Major policy conferences are held throughout the year, from which papers are published thrice yearly in the *Cato Journal*. The Institute also publishes the quarterly magazine *Regulation*.

In order to maintain its independence, the Cato Institute accepts no government funding. Contributions are received from foundations, corporations, and individuals, and other revenue is generated from the sale of publications. The Institute is a nonprofit, tax-exempt, educational foundation under Section 501(c)3 of the Internal Revenue Code.

CATO INSTITUTE
1000 Massachusetts Ave., N.W.
Washington, D.C. 20001